THE MAKING OF MODERN

Britain

A Short History

THE MAKING
OF MODERN
Britain

A Short History

By JOHN BARTLET BREBNER
AND ALLAN NEVINS
Columbia University

W · W · NORTON & COMPANY · INC · *New York*

First Edition

PRINTED IN THE UNITED STATES OF AMERICA
FOR THE PUBLISHERS BY THE VAIL-BALLOU PRESS

Contents

Maps

Preface

WHEN in the spring of 1940 the American people saw Holland and Belgium savagely overrun and France struck prostrate, they realized two important facts: that their nation was in greater peril than ever before, and that to save it from this peril, a close collaboration with the British Commonwealth of Nations must be instituted immediately. As Winston Churchill came to power and the British people rallied behind him with magnificent courage, American sympathies were profoundly stirred. The new Prime Minister had a voice like a trumpet call. His declaration that he had nothing to offer but blood, sweat, and tears, his avowal that Britons would fight on the beaches, in the air, and along the streets to the bitter end, his assertion that they would not rest until they had defeated "a monstrous tyranny never surpassed in the dark and lamentable catalogue of human crime" rang in American ears with rousing effect. That summer, while Congress voted stupendous sums for defense and instituted our first peacetime conscription, the United States and Canada effected a military and naval alliance by setting up a Permanent Joint Board on Defense; in exchange for bases, the United States sent Great Britain fifty destroyers; and leaders of both great American parties agreed on a program of all possible aid to Britain short of war. Before the year ended President Roosevelt, in a fireside speech, had declared that America would send "every ounce and every ton of munitions and supplies that we can possibly spare."

It was in these circumstances that Mr. Churchill declared in a speech of August 20, 1940: "These two great organizations of the English-speaking democracies, the British Empire and the United States, will have to be somewhat mixed up in some of their affairs for mutual and general advantage." He added that he viewed the process without misgiving. "Like the Mississippi, it just keeps rolling along. Let it roll. Let it roll on in full flood, inexorable, irresistible, to broader lands and better days." He spoke truly. The Lease-Lend Act was soon commingling the affairs of the two democracies more completely than ever. Unity of action rapidly became evident in a dozen spheres. And when in August, 1941, it was announced that the President and Prime Minister had held their first momentous conference and drawn up the Atlantic Charter, it became clear that the collaboration was not for the wartime crisis alone. It was also for the days of peace to follow; for the two democracies pledged themselves to strenuous and sustained effort, in close partnership, to organize the world for permanent peace, prosperity, and justice. Since then the co-operation of the English-speaking peoples has moved forward with more than the Mississippi's vigor, with "pomp of waters unwithstood." And with it has moved a general comprehension that its maintenance offers indeed the best guaranty of broader hopes and better days.

An enduring co-operation must rest upon understanding. Bearing that fact in mind, both peoples have found that they know too little about each other, and about each other's history. As the Anglo-American partnership is sealed by common suffering and sacrifices, they need to learn more of their common institutions, their joint traditions, their interplay of cultures; more also about their historic differentiations, which if rightly understood may be highly stimulating. Systematic efforts have been undertaken to remedy this deficiency; more systematic, perhaps, in Great Britain than in the United States.

In 1940–41 one of the authors of this book, spending the winter in Great Britain as Harmsworth Professor at Oxford and as general lecturer, journalist, and broadcaster, was asked by Mr. John G. Winant, the American Ambassador, to prepare a brief history of the United States for British schools. That volume, issued by the Oxford Press, was, in cheap format, at once widely used in the secondary schools of the kingdom. In more expensive format, it was widely read by the general public. Its intention was simple. Presenting the essential facts of American history in concrete narrative form, but dwelling upon the primary elements in the American tradition and heritage—democracy, freedom, tolerance, individualism, optimism—it was an effort to show British readers, first, that American history is a highly interesting story; second, that it has far more of complexity, importance, and grandeur than many Europeans suppose; and third, that it presents a unique message to mankind. The cordiality of the reception given this little book was evidence that a need for it existed, and it has since been followed by others from a number of pens.

But it is equally important for Americans to know more about British history; more of the magnificent drama and adventure bound up in the record, and of its cardinal significance in the story of humanity's slow advance towards liberty and tolerance. Of school texts on the subject there is no lack; but without exception they are too long and too formidably fact-crammed to appeal to a general public. Of other volumes on British history it can be said that many are too specialized for broad use, and that almost none has effectively been brought down to date. It is the feeling of the authors that a place exists for a brief, modern, and readable survey of British history, based on the latest scholarship but written for plain Americans. The intention of this book is again simple. It essays to supply the essential facts in concrete narrative form and intelligible patterns. But it tries to show that British history is in signal degree a record of the growth of freedom and representative institutions; of the achievements, under the law, of both individual energy and social enterprise; of the development of a firm insistence on justice, and of adequate mechanisms for securing it on equal terms to all. This book tries to show that many of the American traditions spring directly from British ideas, institutions, and practices.

It is the belief of the authors that as an American is a better citizen for knowing his own history, he will be a better citizen for knowing the elements of British history. Some of our borrowings from Great Britain are fundamental institutions of government. Some are basic practices of law and justice, from jury trial and the habeas corpus down. Some are habits of mind and temper, hardly recognizable until we lay British and American history side by side. Some are more definite. As one of the authors has written elsewhere: "Every American lawyer and jurist is richer because British law is vigorous and the British bar distinguished. Every American man of letters is the gainer when British literature is varied, energetic, and inspired. Every American social worker, knowing that we borrowed the Y.M.C.A., the Salvation Army, the Charity Organization Society, the Settlement House, and the Boy Scouts from England, knows that he takes constant profit from a sturdy British social movement. Every workingman on this side of the ocean owes something to that British Labor movement which so long outstripped our own. Every thoughtful government officer knows that the continuing British traditions of political freedom, tolerance, and incorruptibility lend strength to our own political institutions."

Of this volume the first chapter is the work of Mr. Nevins, while the remainder is the work of Mr. Brebner; but the plan for the book was worked out in collaboration. To Professor Robert L. Schuyler of Columbia University the authors are indebted for helpful counsel and indispensable corrections of error.

JOHN BARTLET BREBNER
ALLAN NEVINS

Columbia University

CHAPTER I

The Significance of British History

BRITISH HISTORY first presents itself to the ordinary American reader as a varicolored pageant, a crowded succession of pictures, some darkly savage, some strenuously heroic, some sunnily peaceful. They are stranger than the scenes of our own history, and hence perhaps more romantic. But for reasons which we feel subconsciously and instinctively, they touch our sympathies more directly than the historical events of any other country. The people who animate these scenes (like ourselves a racial amalgam, a mixture of Celt, Teuton, and Dane, Norman, Fleming, and Jew) are more like our own people in trait and outlook than are those of any Continental nation. Many a tradition, many a custom, many a habit of thought, runs down from this history to touch chords in our own. Its events and forces are mirrored in a literature which is the common possession of all English-speaking peoples. Even our nursery rhymes cluster largely about English life of centuries ago, and our own writers of boys' tales levy heavily on the same stuff that Scott, Kingsley, and Stevenson used. The laws and political ideals which grew out of this experience are closely akin to our own. Viewed simply as a pageant, British history is more quickly and intimately understood than that of other overseas nations—it holds a more immediate meaning.

The best initial approach to this mighty record *is* as a vivid phantasmagoria, a series of tableaux like those with which the British have fitly frescoed the walls of the Commons' Corridor in the Houses of Parliament. For British history, which from Caesar to Winston Churchill covers almost two thousand years, can if presented in textbook style be all too tightly crammed with dry, hard facts. There is more poetry and imagination, more sense of reality, and hence more historical truth, in the pictures; and he who does not appreciate British history first as a pageant—probably the richest pageant unrolled since Rome's—is not likely to appreciate it in any other way.

We may begin with Augustine and his monks, coming before Aethelbert, as Freeman writes, "carrying an image of our Lord on the Cross wrought in silver, and singing litanies as they came"; the simple king refusing to meet them in any house, lest they prove wizards with some spell. We pass to Caedmon writing the first important English poem on the wild, windswept cliff where Hild's monastery rose above the little landlocked harbor of Whitby. We watch King Alfred, driven to bay in the Athelney marshes by the Scandinavian sea rovers, and there holding out at the head of his trusty band with a spirit that reminds us of Washington at Valley Forge. The sun rises on another warlike scene at Hastings, where Taillefer the minstrel rides forth singing and throwing his sword in air to catch it again; while in vain Harold and his strongest followers wield the English ax so as to cut down Norman horse and rider at a single blow. As we see William the Conqueror harrying all northern England, burning houses, stores, crops, and even live animals, "destroying, so far as in him lay, the life of the earth," we think of sadly modern scenes of devastation and bescorched land. But a more constructive vision rises before us in the building of the huge abbey church at Bury St. Edmunds, with Norman and Saxon blending in a new, busy, alert people; the St. Edmundsbury, seat of learning, piety, benevolence, and expert craftsmanship, which Carlyle long afterward extolled in *Past and Present*.

Medieval England is far away, but not too far to touch us with scenes of drama, heroism, and charm. One shows Thomas à Becket as chancellor, feasting earls, barons, and knights at his daily meal, his guests crowded so thickly about his tables that benches did not suffice, and many sat on trusses of hay in winter and green boughs in summer; another shows the same Becket cut down by Tracy and Fitzurse in Canterbury Cathedral, his assassins crying, "The traitor is dead—he will rise no more." Ever memorable is the historical panel which presents King John granting his barons the Great Charter, with words which marked his despotic idea of sovereignty. "Why do they not ask me my kingdom?" he storms. "I will never grant such liberties as will make me a slave"—but he does grant liberties which make the crown the servant of law, and ultimately of the people. Ever memorable, too, is bloody Bannockburn, where the stalwart peasantry of Scotland defeat the panoply of a feudal invader. The chronicle runs into the folly of the Hundred Years' War and the anarchy of the Wars of the Roses. But there are better scenes as well.

We find Chaucer, born of the tradesman class but a typical English gentleman, kind, humorous, and shrewd, superintending (as Clerk of the Works) the repairs of Westminster Palace, and putting the final touches on some of his best tales—those of the Miller, the Cook, the Wife of Bath, the Merchant, and the Friar. A spirited scene shows us John Ball and the Peasant Rising, with a hundred thousand rebels of the village bands meeting Richard II at Mile End, and forcing him to grant charters of amnesty and commutation of servile dues to men who proclaimed that thenceforth they would "be never named nor held for serfs." In the welcome peace that followed the battle of Tewkesbury, we see Caxton setting up his "red pale" or heraldic shield to summon buyers to the printing press and bookshop that he established in the almonry at Westminster. Those who came to the church could have classics as well, and get them "good chepe." And then the end of civil turmoil and the beginning of the Tudors at Bosworth Field; with Stanley taking the dented, battered crown that Richard left hanging on a hawthorn bush, and setting it on Henry's head amid shouts of "God Save King Harry!"

Later it is a characteristic English scene which brings before us William Tyndale, stubbornly announcing to a learned opponent his determination to make the Bible known in the nation's own tongue. "If God spare my life, ere many years I will cause a boy that driveth a plough shall know more of the Scriptures than thou dost!" A direct sequel of the movement he set on foot appears in another immortal section of our pageant—that which shows Latimer and Ridley burning at the stake in Oxford, and lighting up the mossy walls of Balliol College in "such a candle," as Latimer boasted, "as I trust shall never be put out." Not a few similar martyrdoms might be painted; Rowland Taylor, for example, brought from prison to the stake on Oldham Common, and exclaiming as he saw the throng around his place of execution, "Thanked be God, I am even at home." Not unconnected with these scenes is that in which the pompous Armada, its horns seven miles apart, its huge ships looking like gilded and towered castles, comes on a misty, drizzling July afternoon in sight of the English fleet off the Cornish coast—and for a brief hour indulges its contempt of the darting vessels of Drake, Frobisher, and Hawkins. And not without connection is another maritime scene; the departure of a floating village of one hundred and two souls from Plymouth on the *Mayflower*, with that singing of Psalms in which Edward Winslow tells us the Pilgrims were wont to make "joyful melody in our hearts."

From this point onward the ordinary reader will find more that is familiar in British history, and more that reminds him of the modern British character as he knows it. Until 1776, indeed, British and American history run in a common stream. We feel this as we watch Ralegh eating his last breakfast and smoking his last pipe of Virginia tobacco in the Gatehouse at Westminster, cracking jest after jest as he prepares for his execution in Palace Yard. We feel it as we think of young Milton playing sedately on his organ; Hampden borne, fainting from his wounds, off the field at Chalgrove; and Cromwell, with twenty musketeers at his back, driving the Long Parliament out of its chamber with scornful words—"Begone! Give way to honester men!" There is John Bunyan, weeping in Bedford Jail at the thought of the hardships his little blind daughter might undergo, and writing of how the Pilgrim struggled through the Slough of Despond and past Doubting Castle to the Heavenly City. Especially poignant to one great American sect are the scenes which show the Covenanters persisting in their fierce presbyterianism even as the Stuart soldiery hunt their leaders down like menacing beasts. Particularly pleasant to another sect is the picture of Wesley beginning his revival with a knot of Oxford lads whose regularity in morals, religious observances, and good works made them seem the embodiment of method. Lovers of constitutional liberty will never forget that bit of pageantry which reveals the sixty ships of William III disembarking his troops on the sandy shore of Devon to march through a country jubilant over the end of an outworn dynasty and an outworn era. Nor will lovers of parliamentary development pass by the picture of Robert Walpole, coarse of manners, ignorant of letters and art, managing with consummate dexterity a legislature that had shaken off the royal prerogative and had just begun to learn the power of public opinion.

And then comes suddenly the remarkable expansion of British dominion. Clive at Arcot, himself aiming one of the fieldpieces which enabled the little fort to throw back overwhelming numbers; Wolfe at Quebec, crying as he was struck the third time, "Hold me up—don't let my brave fellows see me drop"; and Phillips sitting in the stern sheets of his small boat, the first European to explore Sydney's magnificent harbor. This was matched by expansion into another field, the beginnings of which are sufficiently indicated by a Glasgow scene that James Watt has himself sketched. "I had gone to take a walk on a fine Sabbath afternoon. I had entered the Green by the gate at the foot of Charlotte Street, and had passed the old washing-house. I was thinking upon the engine at the time, and had gone as far as the herd's house, when the idea came into my mind. . . ." That idea was of the condenser which multiplied the efficiency of the steam engine and helped usher in the industrial revolution.

But pictures, however essential and suggestive, are but an elementary part of history. As we look back across the centuries of the British past, we must try to draw from the multifariously crowded record some conclusions as to its larger significance. For Britain, thanks to various circumstances—her mixture of stocks, her insular situation, her relative freedom from fear of invasion, her natural wealth in coal and iron, her special advantages of position for maritime effort, trade, and colonization—has developed a peculiar character and certain peculiar institutions.

What first strikes us in surveying British history is its *continuity.* The British have had their share of daring innovators; but as a people they like to attain their objectives by a series of logical, moderate steps, rather than by upheavals that break sharply with the past. In this they bear a resemblance to the ancient Romans of republican days, who also preferred evolution to revolution. It is significant that in the political sphere the two greatest revolutionary leaders of British blood were Oliver Cromwell and George Washington, neither of whom could by any stretch of language be termed radical. Cromwell labored earnestly to maintain most of the ancient forms and institutions of the land; and when his son and successor proved incapable of infusing them with authority and power, the British people repudiated the republican regime. The "Glorious Revolution" of 1688 typified the English love of continuity even in change. It was a brief and bloodless readjustment which altered both the monarch and the monarch's position, but kept close to the legitimate line of descent and to the fundamental tenets of the Constitution. Nothing like the French or the Russian revolutions is to be found in British history; nothing so frenzied, sweeping, or decisive in its cleavage between two eras.

This continuity of British history arises in part from the dislike of the people for abrupt and radical change. It arises in still larger part from the fact that in British history a great dominant theme lies full in view—the growth of civil and political liberty. Of this we shall say more in a moment.

But it must be clearly understood that it is not only in political affairs that the British have achieved their progress by slowly broadening down from precedent to precedent. Their social, intellectual, and religious history presents the same emphasis upon a comparatively steady, evolutionary type of advance. The Anglican church is a logical product of patriotic and religious forces working towards a natural fusion. The greatest of the British contributions to scientific thought, the orderly mechanics of Newton and the evolutionary doctrines of Darwin, fit precisely the general British cast of mind. And the "revolution" by which the British did most to remake the world was not effected by marching armies; it was the industrial revolution of sliding pistons and whirring machines.

One element in this continuity of national history is a quality which has stamped the British temper in nearly every relationship: the love of compromise. All countries have their alternations of reform and reaction, progressivism and inertia. Great Britain has no more escaped them than has America. But the British gift for compromise has made it possible to avoid convulsive oscillations, and to maintain a fairly constant reconciliation between old and new. Since the nation reached maturity, its most advanced thinkers or daring spirits—Simon de Montfort, Sir Thomas More, John Pym, Harry Vane, John Locke, William Wilberforce, Robert Owen, Peel, Mill, Lloyd George, Sir William Beveridge—have sought to pull the country forward, or have represented forces that did so; the nation's conservative leaders, with entrenched interests in support, have resisted them; and in general workable compromises have been hammered out. In modern times it has been the essence of this compromise that the minority should not resist the majority by violent or illegal acts, and that the majority should not abuse its authority over the minority. In other lands extremes of repression have bred extremes of revolt, and *vice versa*. In Britain the ruling principle has rather been one of moderation, conciliatory adjustment, and willingness to wait upon the slow evolution of opinion.

In due time the British Constitution came to represent not only a series of compromises, but a set of theoretical balances; and in imitation of this theory, the makers of the American Constitution finally carried balance to a new pitch of completeness. The British state church represented, in considerable degree, a compromise between Catholicism and Protestantism. It is evidence of the persistent spirit of compromise that the first great factory-reform legislation came from three men, Michael Sadler, Richard Oastler, and Lord Ashley, who were Tories and opponents of radical democracy. It is evidence of the same spirit that the majority which imposed slave emancipation upon the colonies showed its fairness to a minority interest by compensating the owners. On a still more impressive stage, the spirit of moderate adjustment was again exhibited when Britain, in making peace with the defeated Boers, gave them a liberal grant of money for rehabilitation, and made promises of self-government which were carried out to the letter within the next few years.

These special virtues of the British record, it must be admitted, are not dramatic, and may even seem tame. There are periods in history when a dazzling new illumination, a sudden *éclaircissement,* springs from the impetuous release of energy in some nation. So it was when Christianity made its advent into a world to which Roman law and Greco-Roman thought had just given unprecedented unity. Such an illumination came again when from southern Europe shot up the rosy effulgence of the Renaissance. It came once more in the new birth of humanitarianism, idealism, and passionate love of liberty which the French Revolution gave to mankind—a dawn in which one British poet thought it bliss to be alive. British history presents no spectacles of this sort. For all her geniuses (and the world has produced none greater than Shakespeare and Newton), for all her energy, Great Britain has never exploded a sheaf of rockets over the pathway of humanity, illuminating the pinnacles far ahead. Instead, she has offered a sober, steady, and for the most part admirably clear light upon immediate problems. She has been content if her contributions to civilization were realistic, dependable, and practically useful.

Men who by temperament like instant and energetic reform, who are impatient of any but radical changes, and who admire the French and Russian revolutions for their clean sweep of old abuses, may find something distasteful in the strong lines of continuity and compromise in British history. In gradualness they see stubborn resistance to change. They point to the long grip maintained on the British government by the unreformed and unrepresentative Parliament of the eighteenth and early nineteenth centuries; to the fifty years of dreadful suffering among the masses which followed the first onset of the industrial revolution. They are horrified by the wide gap which developed between rich and poor as the industrial revolution approached completion—by the two Englands that, as Disraeli said, were so foreign to one another. Taking the point of view of Thomas Jefferson and William Morris, they assert that a little revolution now and then is good for any nation. It would have been better, they hold, had Britain sometimes given rein to a fierce revolt against "the power that helps not," the "wisdom that teacheth not." Too much, they say, of Tennyson's slow growth of freedom under crowning common sense; it was *too* slow.

But here it is necessary to point out that alongside the continuity and moderation which mark all modern British history there has run a great deal of fiery individual energy and even revolt. In fact, the great triumph of British compromise is the reconciliation of individualism, of free enterprise, with law. It is not for lack of physical or intellectual daring that the British have avoided mass revolutions. They can achieve their end in other ways; while they regard mass revolts as herdlike and irrational affairs. In all British history, down to the page written by the R.A.F. ("never before did so many owe so much to so few"), the individual has counted for more than in neighboring lands. When we read British history we see at once that it has to an uncommon degree been made by self-willed, hardy, resourceful characters. The typical Englishman has stood on his own feet; he has shown an energy and self-reliance that made him a good explorer, colonizer, and trader. He did not subject himself to Napoleons or Hitlers. He had a maxim about his house being his castle. He liked to form his own opinion and utter it stoutly, as Latimer did when he gave Henry VIII a copy of the Vulgate marked at a passage denouncing the king's own vices. It was long ago remarked that each of these islanders tended to be an island in himself. "They are good lovers, good haters, slow but obstinate admirers, and in all things very much steeped in their temperament," wrote Emerson. Their individualism, distrusting mob action as it distrusted other forms of tyranny, lent itself to change by un-co-ordinated if fairly steady effort.

And it should also be pointed out that, if he has sometimes seemed slow, the Briton on the whole has moved as fast and as far in his reforms as any other people. The weakness of violence lies not only in its hectic character, but in its impermanence. The French Revolution, sweeping away much evil, also destroyed much good; while it unquestionably brought about reactions that undid much of its work. The Russian Revolution overshot its mark, and a more sober readjustment became necessary. But if the British have moved slowly, they have moved steadily. The British state, Burke wrote when he condemned the French Revolution, was unquestionably that which pursued the greatest variety of ends, and was the least disposed to sacrifice any one of them to the others. "It aims at taking in the entire circle of human desires, and securing for them their fair enjoyment." Accepting this as a sound aim, we can credit Britain with achieving really balanced reforms as rapidly and effectively as any country of equally complex problems.

For if vested privilege and deep-rooted abuses died hard in Britain, they die hard everywhere. Long the stronghold of *laissez faire,* Great Britain first modified and then repudiated it with a vigor which left the more richly endowed and therefore more comfortable American republic far behind. To that part of *laissez faire* which made self-interest the dynamo of progress, the British clung. But the factory legislation of the nineteenth century cut deeply into the Victorian Compromise. Then came the renaissance of the Liberal party early in the twentieth century, and a series of laws which, from the standpoint of more conservative nations like the United States, at first seemed socialistic and revolutionary. They included laws which pensioned the aged, insured workers against unemployment and sickness, compensated the victim of industrial accidents, placed trade unions on a protected level, attacked the slums by state housing and town planning, abolished sweated labor, and finally, by a daring series of tax measures, equalized income to such a degree that the whole of the immense rise in income during the second World War passed into the pockets of the poor. The people themselves had meanwhile set up schemes of co-operation that found few rivals elsewhere. British social legislation, the work of Liberal, Labor, and Conservative ministries alike, was moderate and orderly in method, but deeply radical in effect. It had lifted the British toiler to a higher and securer level than his French brother occupied, for all the effects of the French Revolution. It had given the British masses far more freedom and safety than were enjoyed by the beneficiaries of the Russian Revolution. In short, the British method had by any standard of comparison justified itself.

But if continuity, moderation, and a talent for progress by compromise and evolution are the special traits of British history, what have they done for the world at large? In answering this question we come to that before-mentioned theme which helps so much to give unity to British history —the development of civil liberty and political freedom. Through many centuries this one motif imparts meaning to the British record, and infuses itself into nearly all its elements.

The Middle Ages, which bequeathed to most countries an authoritarian type of government, endowed the British peoples with certain seeds of freedom. The Great Charter required the king to keep the law, and provided that he might be compelled to do so. Not only had Parliament gained an early and useful existence, but by the end of the thirteenth century it had partially established its exclusive right to lay taxes. In the next century it even began to enforce the responsibility of the ministers of the crown to itself. But the long era of the Tudors brought a relapse towards authoritarian models, and the frail plant of liberty for a time seemed in danger of shriveling to death. The doctrine of the divine right of the sovereign had to be overthrown. A larger degree of representative government had to be won, and the clear supremacy of the House of Commons to be established. The struggle was protracted and dangerous. But whereas in the reign of Elizabeth at the end of the sixteenth century authoritarianism was still firmly planted, by the reign of William and Mary, at the end of the seventeenth, freedom was won. The fortresses of bigotry, intolerance, and personal tyranny had been captured, and some of the outworks of special privilege stormed. A great work of liberation had been largely completed.

The heroes of the contest are names honored wherever political freedom lives: the fearless Algernon Sidney; the greathearted Harrington; the shaggy, burly, forthright Pym; Hampden of ship-money fame; the poet-pamphleteer John Milton; the iron Cromwell; Hobbes, who taught that the origin of political power resides in the people; his pupil Locke, who asserted the right of the people to resist tyranny, and the supremacy of Parliament as the embodiment of the people's will—these and many more. And they did more than overthrow the authoritarian evils of the past; they built for the future. They set up the doctrine that government by public discussion and general public agreement is the only really stable government. Representative institutions should express popular opinion, and the chosen legislature of the land should have the final voice in all political affairs. Henceforth an increased orderliness characterized British affairs. By an intermittent but inexorable succession of steps the fabric of self-government was consolidated and made more democratic—the Mutiny Act, which give Parliament control over the army; the firm assertion of Parliamentary control over the purse; the rise of the cabinet system; and repeated extensions of the franchise.

The greater part of this development occurred in time to enable British colonists to transplant the system to new lands overseas. Representative government, indeed, was immediately exported, and the export was maintained; so that it came to flourish in all parts of the English-speaking world, and in parts which, like Quebec and India, were hardly English-speaking at all. When Virginia and Massachusetts were planted, it was accepted that such colonies must have some form of representative government. What was more, it was agreed that their representatives should control the taxes levied in the colonies. Not only on the American mainland, but in Bermuda and the West Indian islands as well, sturdy legislatures sprang up. Lord Mansfield ruled in the eighteenth century that the crown could not legislate by orders in council in any colony possessing British settlers and a representative legislature, even if that colony were obtained by conquest. And the American colonies were soon asserting that even Parliament could never legislate for them; that none but their own elected assemblies could do that.

At first, to be sure, the export of political freedom was incomplete. Representative legislatures were set up overseas; but the other great British agency of self-government, the executive responsible to the legislature, was not. Instead, the crown appointed the governors. Partly for this reason, Washington was soon carrying the ideas of Vane and Hampden to the battlefield, and Jefferson was writing those of Locke into the Declaration of Independence. "In George Washington we honor the principles he vindicated against ourselves," asserts a British historian. But responsible cabinet government was finally established in Canada in 1847, and the example was shortly followed elsewhere. Thus the Dominions grew into nationhood with replicas of the British system, each co-ordinating its representative legislature with a responsible executive—Canada, Australia, South Africa, New Zealand, and Eire. Even parts of India were so endowed. And thus British ideas of political liberty and representative government spread around the globe.

But of equal importance was the British contribution to that modern ideal of civil liberty so warmly cherished by democratic states. Arbitrary governmental acts, depriving the individual of the rights of free speech, free association, a free press, and free justice, were abhorrent to most Britons when they were still accepted as inevitable throughout the greater part of Europe. Arrest by secret warrant, as in France down to 1789, and in Germany under Hitler; imprisonment and punishment by "administrative process," as in Russia under the Czars; close control of newspapers, books, and public gatherings, as in all totalitarian countries—such abuses Britons early found intolerable. The Great Charter, the Petition of Right, the Habeas Corpus Act, the Bill of Rights, were the landmarks of the process by which personal liberty was made secure. By 1690 the struggle had been completely won, and despite some periods of tension and turmoil, it remained won. "All civilized governments," the *Edinburgh Review* stated in 1807, "may be divided into free and arbitrary; or more accurately, into the government of England and the other European governments." That sounds like a mistimed boast, for the first decades of the nineteenth century were not the happiest era of British liberties. Yet it was essentially true. The French historian Halévy declares that not only were the words true for 1807, but they would have been equally true for 1815. The Swiss historian Edouard Fueter offers the same testimony: "Freedom of discussion existed to an extent which was unthinkable in any other country."

A noble part of British history clusters about the process by which civil liberties were defined and secured. A still finer part clusters about the heroic acts of men who vindicated them when attacked, or extended their application. When free speech and free publication were threatened by Crown and Ministry, John Wilkes became a popular hero by defending them—and ultimately triumphed over all opponents. In a period of general reaction, Wilberforce and his associates halted the slave trade, and, largely by public meetings and the use of monster petitions, took the first step toward striking the shackles from the Negro. Efforts to interfere with the utterances of journalists like William Cobbett and Leigh Hunt simply lifted them to greater notice and prestige than ever. An unshakable tradition was built up by which liberty of the person, the pen, and the voice were almost completely protected. Great Britain became a haven of safety for the exiled revolutionists of all Europe. From her soil Herzen spoke to Russia, Mazzini to Italy, Victor Hugo to France, Kossuth to Hungary, and Karl Marx to the world. And meanwhile the British concept of civil liberty had inevitably and irresistibly radiated its influence throughout a great part of the world.

When British colonists went overseas—many of them escaping from political, economic, and ecclesiastical restrictions—they carried with them ideas of civil freedom and religious toleration. New commonwealths were founded, like Rhode Island and Pennsylvania, Maryland and Georgia, on the assumption that diverse faiths might worship freely together. When colonial charters were drawn up, the British ideas of free speech, the right of petition, and habeas corpus were written into or implied in them. So ingrained were these principles in the minds of English-speaking folk that when the Convention of 1788 omitted them from the American Constitution, popular clamor forced the speedy addition of a Bill of Rights; for everybody called the first ten amendments by the good old British term. And another agency, the British common law, helped in the diffusion of civil liberties. As distinguished from Roman civil law, it has gone to every part of the United States save Louisiana, and every part of the British Commonwealth except Quebec, South Africa, and Ceylon. The primary concern of this common law is with basic human rights. Its diffusion means that over a large part of the globe, jurists have the same general idea of what these rights are, and interpret the law affecting them by the light of a universally respected body of precedents.

Civil liberty and free political institutions—these are the inestimable legacy which Great Britain has bequeathed to our age and the ages to come. We can partly explain how she was able to make so valuable a bequest. The insular position of the country rendered a burdensome military establishment unnecessary; this fact obviated any growth of the odious militaristic abuses long common in France, and still longer in Prussia; while the unlikelihood of much connivance between external and internal enemies reduced the temptation to repressive measures. As British resources were developed, the superior average standard of living (always higher than on the Continent) lessened the fear of disorders and mob outbreaks; and this again made for freedom. The growth of commerce and colonization, with maritime connections all over the globe, broadened the outlook of Britons; for the sea has always been a natural teacher of liberty. Once the habit of compromise was estab-

lished, it too had its effect. Men might clamor for redress
of grievances, but so long as nobody demanded revolution
as a fundamental principle, harsh countermeasures were
unnecessary. It is in countries where revolt is constantly
feared, as in the Russia of Nicholas and the Germany of
Hitler, that civil liberty is crushed under bayonets. The
increasing homogeneity of the British people, another consequence of their insular position, also counted for tolerance and mutual respect. But not all the factors explaining
Britain's special contribution to free government and human rights can be enumerated. When we have finished,
something must still be attributed to a vague but very real
entity in the background.

This entity is the character of the British people; a character that, after all, is the best gift of Britain to the world,
and the most significant fact of British history. What is life
to a man, or history to a nation, if they do not produce
character? And what nation has a more distinct, a better-
balanced, or a tougher-fibered character than the British?
Of course this entity is difficult to define. It has varied
somewhat from age to age, the British character in the
time of Gladstone and Tennyson being perceptibly different from the English character in the days of Elizabeth and
Shakespeare. Unquestionably, too, it has been modified by
classes and social groups; the character of the squirearchy,
the aristocracy, the factory hands, and the tradesmen all
differing very clearly. But however elusive of definition, a
composite national character does exist, and few will quarrel as to its chief elements. Milton said that the principal
aim of government and social institutions should be "to
train up a nation in true wisdom and virtue, and that which
springs from thence, magnanimity." This was the Puritan
ideal. Other men held other ideals. But in the end some

wisdom, a great deal of virtue, and a truly remarkable amount of magnanimity did get into the British character.

The British themselves, by their educational system, by the special codes of a stratified society, and by traditions and principles that are constantly impressed upon the national consciousness, have treated character as their proudest possession. No people has more powerfully instilled the precept of duty. It was the theme of Addison in the quotation so beloved by Washington: " 'Tis not in mortals to command success, but we'll do better, Brutus, we'll deserve it." It was the theme of Wordsworth in the lines on the happy warrior so often quoted by Woodrow Wilson. It was the theme of Tennyson in the verses so familiar to an older American generation: "Not once or twice, in our great island story, the path of duty was the way to glory." And the precept, eloquently stated by the poets, has been gallantly illustrated in the lives of men both humble and conspicuous. We can all think of the modern instances: Scott at the South Pole, Mallory and Irvine marching to their death in the mists that capped Mount Everest, the plain soldiers on the beach at Dunkirk. The steadfast adherence to duty has meant a special insistence upon steadfast integrity in general. The Spaniards have a proverb for truth —"on the word of an Englishman." In the Orient, the very peoples who dislike the English most strongly nevertheless place implicit confidence in their honor and reliability as administrators. There is a wise instinct in this national emphasis on dutiful character. It is not in itself more important than intellect. But there is not much that a nation can do to guarantee itself a special endowment of brains— though by schools and other cultural appliances it can make sure that they are well cultivated. There are ways, on the other hand, by which a nation can definitely give itself character; and the combination of brains and character is as admirable as the spectacle of brains without virtue (illustrated in the temporary perversion of part of the German people) may be terrible.

The British character has its weaknesses, as Britons have confessed, in a widespread tendency towards materialism, a certain readiness to take British superiority for granted, and a general though not universal heedlessness of the unseen, the spiritual, and the subtly artistic. Its cardinal virtues are its vigor, its honesty, its decency, its resourcefulness, its optimism, and its courage. They combine to make up a strength that in time of trial can be stubbornly dauntless—and more than once the world has had reason to lean on that strength. When Pitt said in Napoleonic days that Britain would save herself by her own exertions, and Europe by her example, he was appealing to the British character. When Churchill in a time of unexampled peril called upon Britons to so conduct themselves that future generations would call this their finest hour, he too was challenging the British character. Neither challenge went unanswered; nor, we may be sure, will future challenges fail to meet the same valiant response. The role of Europe in world affairs is being altered and manifestly reduced; the role of Britain in Europe and the world is being changed by forces too vast for any nation to control. But the part played by the British character on this planet is not likely to alter greatly, or to become any the less valuable.

But from the broad significance of British history we must now turn to a detailed examination of the events and forces which shaped it.

CHAPTER II

The Melting Pot

FOR CENTURIES the British Isles were considered to be the
end of the world, that is, the end of an ancient or medieval
world whose center was somewhere in the Mediterranean
basin—in Greece or Egypt or at Constantinople or Rome.
The civilized peoples of the warm Mediterranean countries, if they happened to know that the British Isles existed
at all, thought of their barbarian inhabitants as living near
Ultima Thule—Farthest North—among volcanoes, ice-
bergs, and the mouths of Hell.

When one looks at a map or globe of today there seems
to be at least some justification for those old ideas. The
islands do lie between the same latitudes as the bleak coast
of Labrador and the subarctic Kamchatka Peninsula. Yet
in the North Atlantic, as in the North Pacific, persistent
ocean currents and winds make the eastern margins very
much warmer than the western. The British Isles have
much the same moist, temperate climate as the Pacific coast
of North America between northern California and Alaska.
They never become yellow and brown with winter as do
regions much farther south elsewhere, for frost and snow
seldom last for long, and abundant, intermittent rains
make much of the landscape green and parklike all year
round. The ever-present woods and meadows and hedge-
rows of "England's green and pleasant land" form a back-

ground and framework for the fertile cultivated fields and for the massed buildings of the industrial and urban centers.

There is little that is violently dramatic in the appearance of the British Isles. Most of England is less than four hundred feet above sea level and the hills seldom rise above a thousand feet except in the west (Cornwall and Wales), or in the central spine of the island which reaches down from mountainous Scotland. The highest mountain in England and Wales is Snowdon (3560 feet), and Scotland's moor-topped mountains seldom rise above four thousand feet or Ireland's above three thousand. The endlessly varied contours of these islands are for the most part gentle and rounded, worn smooth by time. Nature rouses the emotions only by the thunder of the seas along the coasts, the eerie emptiness of the water-soaked, infertile moors, and the uninterrupted areas of low, but veritable, mountains in Wales and Scotland and Ireland.

Everywhere in England and the lowlands of Scotland and Ireland are rivers, leisurely streams which must have been comparatively placid and well behaved even before men curbed and controlled them for drainage and transportation. Each year they flood and fertilize the meadows along their banks, but they give the impression of having followed the same shallow, winding courses since the beginning of recorded time. Great Britain has no Mississippis or Missouris capable of carving out new channels and leaving former river towns stranded far from the new banks. Her many lakes and ponds are on the same scale, small catch basins among the hills and mountains rather than sprawling inland seas like those of Asia, Africa, and the Americas.

England, where most of the population is concentrated, is a small region, a sort of triangle whose base, close to the

Continent, is about three hundred miles long and whose sides, reaching up to Scotland, are about fifty miles longer. The total area is approximately that of Illinois. No part of these islands can be very far from the sea, and their natural center, London, can be reached from almost any point within a day by train, or in two or three hours by air.

If the men of the Mediterranean were wrong about the British climate, they were right about the islands being the last outpost of their world. The British Isles lean outward into the North Atlantic, separated from the great land mass of Europe and Asia by the shallow English Channel. While it seems likely that the twenty-mile interval between Dover and Cap Gris Nez was dry land in earlier geological periods, and that the Thames joined the Rhine on its way to the Atlantic, yet it would be hard to exaggerate the importance in British history of the moat which has spared the islands from the unremitting responsibility of land frontiers. Even before the islanders learned how to put a navy on the surrounding waters, the choppy Channel funnel of winds and tides was a formidable obstacle for those who cast envious eyes on England.

And yet substantial numbers crossed at intervals from as long ago as we can find record down to the eleventh century, so that England was for untold centuries a stopping place for successive waves of human beings on the march across Europe. Some of them were fugitives before groups more powerful than they, some were raiders who liked the British Isles better than their own homelands, and some were empire builders from the Continent; but, whatever they were, there was no place farther on to go to until the Atlantic crossing was learned. Each wave of people which broke across the Channel merged with the stock already there to form the human blend which we know today.

Archeologists have discovered the traces of man in Britain during the Old Stone Age, the New Stone Age, and the Bronze Age, that is, from man's first recorded existence on earth down to about 1800 B.C. They have also found evidences that British pearls, jet, tin, copper, and gold were exchanged for products from Spain, the Levant, and Egypt, thousands of years before the beginning of the Christian era. That was in the days of the so-called Iberians in England, dark-haired men who were a mixture of southern and middle European stocks and who made the long progress from chipped stone implements to bronze, who tilled the soil and kept animals, who wove cloth and built boats, and who created magnificent earthwork fortifications and reared imposing places of worship such as Stonehenge. Like the Indians and the pioneering whites of North America, they made their footpaths across the island close under the ridges of the hills, particularly the chalk downs, where the soil was drained, the waterways small, and the blanket of forest thinned out or even absent.

These folk were supplanted, submerged, or pushed into the uplands by successive tribal waves of tall, fair-haired Celts who kept crossing the Channel into the British Isles from the seventh to the third centuries before Christ. Their mastery of iron working gave them a decisive advantage which delivered the islands into their hands. Of the Celts, the Gaels seem to have come first, to be followed by the Cymri and Britons. Always the strongest tribes seized the south and east of England, pushing their predecessors farther on. By the time that Julius Caesar crossed the Channel in 55 B.C., the Iberians formed the bulk of the population in Cornwall, Wales, Ireland, and the Scottish Highlands, and the Roman empire builder had to deal with Celtic Britons in the south and east. He came over to subdue them be-

cause of the aid and refuge which they had been giving to
their kinsmen in northern Gaul (France) who were resist-
ing the Roman occupation there. He made two punitive
raids, but Roman conquest did not begin until Claudius
invaded Britain with 40,000 men in A.D. 43.

The Romans gradually took over Britain as far north as
the Scottish Highlands in their usual efficient way, but
scholars believe that, while the quality of Roman occupation was what had become usual elsewhere in Europe, the
quantity, or sheer weight, of the enterprise was somewhat
below normal. The fighting Britons, of course, were in the
long run no match for the disciplined Roman soldiery, who
killed many of them in battle, forced others out of the fertile lowlands to get along as best they could with the
previous inhabitants of Cornwall, Wales, Ireland, and Scotland, and harnessed the remainder to the peaceful exploitation of the most fertile and productive parts of Britain. The
Romans laid down over the land a network of orderly garrisons and of stone roads whose beeline routes can still be
traced.[1] They built immense stone walls in the north to
keep out the Gaelic Picts and Scots, and they maintained a
special military and naval organization in the southeast as
a warning to restless people from northern Europe who
might otherwise have considered Britain an easy mark.

The Roman Peace which was imposed on Britain for
almost four hundred years did make the island tempting to
marauders. The well-planned and well-built garrison towns
and trading centers meant concentrations of goods and
money on a scale unattainable by nomads, and the beauti-
fully laid out and admirably managed Roman country
estates (*villae*) seemed to represent a gracious way of life

[1] English place names ending in "chester" (*castra*) mark the sites of Roman garrisons.

which was little calculated to produce warrior peoples. The new Christian religion which was making headway during the third and fourth centuries also had softening effects. Only the professional Roman legionaries stood between aggressive Nordic tribes of northern Europe and a magnificent temptation to loot.

When Rome declined and the ancient capital, instead of pumping out energies through the arteries of empire, began to suck in the legions and their generals to compete in Italy for the office of emperor, such outer margins as Britain felt the effects at once. Sometimes the troops in Britain set out for Gaul or Rome to make their leader emperor; sometimes they repudiated the emperor of the day and Britain became a separate principality for a time. We do not know much of the details of Roman disintegration in Britain, but they may easily be imagined. The Nordic barbarians were constantly probing to discover the soft spots in the islands' defenses, and, when the legions were called home at the end of the fourth century, they poured in upon the somewhat helpless Romanized Celts from every direction. Up in the north, the un-Romanized Picts and Scots and, in the west, the Welsh and Irish Gaels scented the same prey.

Four centuries of *Pax Romana,* six and a half centuries of Nordic invasions—the time scale of British history at the beginning of the Christian era is almost impossible to grasp. The period between the first Roman invasion and the last substantial Nordic invasion (that of the Normans in 1066) was almost four times as long as the entire period of white settlement in Canada and the United States. Since most of the Nordic invaders were illiterate, our knowledge of their doings for six hundred and fifty years is decidedly fragmentary. Yet they were the effective frontiersmen of British history, who hunted the game, cleared the forests

for their fields and meadows, put the land into tillage and
animal husbandry, and fought, almost continuously, both
among themselves and against successive waves of invasion.
For want of a better name they have been called Anglo-
Saxons, and it was they who, after making the British Isles
their own, launched forth the English-speaking peoples to
the four corners of the earth.

A convenient way to picture this troubled six hundred
and fifty years is to think of the period as divided into two—
a preliminary series of destructive waves of conquest
launched against Romanized Britain and then another series of desperate defenses of the conquered areas against
unending new waves of attack. No doubt the process began
along the low southern and eastern coasts of the island
where the tidal estuaries of slow rivers furnished convenient entries for the long ships of the northern warriors.
Other regions were harder nuts to crack; in fact, Cornwall,
Wales, Ireland, and Scotland have substantially retained
to this day the mingled Iberian and Celtic stocks which
occupied them in Roman times. The British Isles did not
present a uniform picture at any one time, but instead all
the different stages of conquest, settlement, local war, and
defense against invaders, depending largely upon the vulnerability of any given region to attack.

We know from the heroic poems of the European Nordic
peoples how they conducted their warlike lives in their
homelands beside the Baltic and the North Sea. Around an
outstanding leader and fighter, ambitious warriors would
group themselves, pledging unconditional loyalty to him
in return for a share of the spoils which they won and for a
place in the hall which he maintained for them in the intervals of their warfare. These men were the aristocracy of
their peoples, whose only profession was fighting. When

not at war, they displayed their prowess in hunting, carousing, and exchanging "tall tales" of warfare and adventure. Below them in the social scale were free farmers, who might also bear arms in time of emergency, and many others, half-free or slaves, who were not allowed to carry weapons and whose labors as tillers of the soil, herdsmen, woodsmen, weavers, cooks, and artisans, supported the fighting men whose code did not allow them to stoop to ordinary toil.

Such a leader and his band, in one or more narrow, shallow, open ships, propelled for the most part by oars and carrying from twenty to sixty men, would set out in the spring for adventure in Britain. Tradition says that some of them were invited in by the unwarlike Britons to protect them against the Gaels, but even if this be true the basic consideration was that a rich island lay open before them. It is now believed that during the fifth century the raiders combined in great "hosts" to sweep across broad belts of the island, laying waste everything before them and returning home with their loot and their captives. During these times only the legendary British King Arthur seems to have been able to organize for a short time sufficiently stubborn resistance to make a shadowy name for himself in history. Since the invaders were incapable of maintaining the buildings, the agriculture, or the commerce of this Romanized land, they destroyed its cities and villas and subsequently avoided these sites as places in which to live. The period of mere waste and destruction may have lasted for fifty or a hundred years in much of the south and the Midlands, while remnants of the Celtic population found refuge in the woods and uplands or fled across the Channel to Brittany.

Yet Britain was obviously too tempting a land to be left waste. Its climate, its rich soil and great forests, made it greatly preferable to the rocky margins of the Baltic or the forbidding sandy soil, moors, and marshes on the shores of the North Sea. Even warriors could see the advantages of a move from the Continent to Britain and in groups of varying size they chose suitable sites for settlement. These areas they seem to have divided up into substantial blocks as great estates for the military aristocracy and free warriors, but their actual cultivation was the work of land workers ranging from freemen to slaves, many of whom were transported from the Continent, but some of whom were conquered Britons. Once under way, the migration from the Continent grew rapidly until by its sheer mass it obliterated almost all traces of Rome and of the Celts from the most desirable parts of the island. Only the indestructible Roman roads remained, never to be adequately replaced until the eighteenth century.

The annals of Anglo-Saxon England from the beginnings of settlement to the Norman Conquest form a confused pattern of the rise and decline of regional principalities and kingdoms, interminable wars against newcomers from North Germany and Scandinavia, and the gradual emergence of the idea and the actuality of a single Kingdom of England. There was little natural unity. Even when the largest groups of Jutes, Angles, and Saxons were united under single leaders, there were enough varieties of each to make seven separate kingdoms. Even the geographical unity of the island area failed to create a national unit, for communications were poor, the Celts could not be rooted out of the western and northern highlands, and the surrounding seas were highways for invasion.

The Christian church proved to be of great help in teaching the Anglo-Saxons something about political unity. The new religion was brought to bear upon them from two

directions. In Scotland and northern England missionaries
arrived from Ireland, the one part of western Europe where
classical learning and Roman Christianity of the early type
really flourished during the seventh century. The Anglo-
Saxons' primitive, unsystematic faith was no match for the
pure religion and scriptural authority of the Celtic teachers
or for their assured promises of salvation for a life after
death, so that Christianity began to spread southward in
England. Coming to meet it from the south was another
wave of Christianity which had been set going in Kent at
the very end of the sixth century by Augustine, a missionary
sent out by Pope Gregory the Great to win England for the
European Catholic church which he was organizing under
Roman authority. The loosely organized, accommodating
old Celtic church met the crisply organized Roman one in
the Midlands, and a synod at Whitby in 664 accepted Roman direction. Able churchmen were dispatched to the
new field and divided it into parishes, episcopal dioceses,
and two provinces under archbishops at Canterbury and
York. If political unity was lacking, religious unity was not,
and now the long slow business began of teaching an unlet-
tered people that the new religion meant something more
than the excitement and pageantry of the mass baptisms by
which kings customarily led whole peoples into the church.

The churchmen of the seventh and later centuries
brought with them learning, discipline, organizing ability,
and the shrewd realization that they had much to gain from
making the Anglo-Saxon kingship amount to something.
They took over the matter of crowning and anointing kings
in order to set them apart from ordinary men; they used
their ability to read and write for setting up royal administrations and records; and they induced Anglo-Saxon kings
and magnates to write down the accepted customs of the

folk, or dooms, in imitation of Roman law. They acquired
property and not only managed it skillfully, but secured
deeds or charters for it which laymen were quick to demand
for themselves. Above all, since the church never died,
their efforts did a great deal to give continuity to kingship,
royal administration, law, and land tenure.

Early in the ninth century, Wessex, the kingdom of the
West Saxons whose capital was at Winchester, acquired formal overlordship over most of England and Wales, but almost immediately it had to face unremitting pressure from
the Danes or Vikings, skillful seafarers and land warriors
from Norway, Denmark, and Sweden. These men almost
conquered the island, coming at it from all directions, but
they were finally checked by Alfred the Great about 878.
During the next twenty years he made headway against
them, as did his successors, so that in the tenth century, even
in the northern and eastern regions which the Danes had
made their own, they accepted Christianity and the Wessex
kingship and adapted their own institutions to settled *English* life. Yet, with hordes of unruly Scandinavian seafarers
ever ready to attack, the English kingship was still a precarious thing, depending as it did so heavily on the qualities of the king. By the eleventh century it was apparent
that England was still a prize to be seized by the strongest
because its peoples had failed in the course of six hundred
years to rally round a national administration through
which they could effectively exert their native strength.

During the first half of the eleventh century two outside
forces contended for the British Isles. After two centuries
of glorious seafaring which had carried them from the
Baltic to North America and from Dublin [2] to Constan-

2 Which, with Wexford, Waterford, Cork, and Limerick, was founded by
the Vikings.

tinople, raiding, trading, and establishing great settlements,
the Scandinavian Vikings erected a short-lived empire.
Sweyn Forkbeard, king of Denmark, and his son Canute
stitched together by war and trade, into one temporary
structure, the British Isles and the Baltic lands and linked
this vast area, by sea and overland through Russia, with
Constantinople, the magnificent capital of the surviving
Eastern or Byzantine half of the Roman Empire. For a
little less than twenty years (say from 1016 to 1035), England was cut off from the main course of European development as it stemmed through the church from Rome, and,
since Canute moved his capital from Denmark to England,
the island people had a foretaste of the maritime empire
which was not to return to them for over five hundred years.

When Canute's worthless sons frittered away their inheritance, and Edward the Confessor of the House of Wessex became monarch of an independent England, he opened
the gates to the second competitor for mastery of England,
the latinized Duchy of Normandy, just across the Channel
and nominally a part of the shaky kingdom of France. Here
a large colony of the same Viking raiders who had almost
conquered England in Alfred's time had settled on the
lower Seine and extended their sway west to Brittany and
east to Picardy and Flanders. They had rapidly absorbed
every advantageous characteristic of the Franco-Roman civilization which they found there. They became French-
speaking Christians, they learned and improved the cavalry
warfare and castle building of a feudal society, and they
amalgamated with their own institutions the superior no-
tions of law and administration which had come down to
the Franks in fragmentary form from Charlemagne, that
great emperor who had temporarily brought most of west·

ern Europe under his sway at the beginning of the ninth century.

The Normans were amazingly vigorous and truly apt, so that by the middle of the eleventh century, under Duke William, they had made themselves the most progressive state in Europe. They were ready and anxious to expand just when England fell into the weak hands of "St. Edward the King," the founder of Westminster Abbey. What Edward admired most in the world was the vigorous monastic revival which he had seen during his exile in Normandy. When he became king he was already more than half a Norman and he could not think of better administrators and church leaders than his Norman friends. His chastity precluded the birth of an heir to the throne; his diffidence as a ruler condemned his England to civil war; in brief, the Norman Conquest began with the coronation in 1042 of the last king of the house of Alfred the Great.

It is true that Edward was succeeded by Harold, the son of Earl Godwin, and that in 1066 King Harold defeated near York a Norwegian attempt at conquest barely in time to come south by forced marches to his defeat at Norman hands, but the basic damage had been done by King Edward. England had no navy with which to break up Duke William's fleet of transports, Anglo-Saxon warriors had not been trained in the new cavalry tactics, and thus it came about that after one stubborn, day-long battle near Hastings, in which Harold was killed, England fell before an invading force of between ten and fifteen thousand men.

The conquest was completed during the next five years by means of an utterly ruthless devastation of the north and east. Large areas were depopulated by massacre or flight, whole villages and towns of wooden buildings were wiped out by fire, and every center of resistance was crushed. Two great monuments commemorate to this day the Norman achievement—the castle and cathedral which look out over the north from the cliff site at Durham, and the lofty cathedral pile which rises above the lowlands of East Anglia from the Isle of Ely. Norman architecture was grim, massive and fortresslike. The Norman Conquest was equally resolute.

Duke William, now King William the Conqueror, at once proceeded to use England as his testing ground for a kind of monarchy which he thought superior to what he saw around him in Europe. If he could make it work in England, he and his dynasty might extend it in other directions from Normandy at the expense of less progressive rulers. In England he had the inestimable advantage of being master and therefore of being able to make a fresh start, but in order to do so he had to manipulate two intractable masses of human material, about a million and a half subjugated Anglo-Saxons, and the few thousand Continental adventurers who had followed in his train. He must somehow fuse them into malleable metal for his design.

The Anglo-Saxons were for the most part frontier farmers who raised grain, hogs, and cattle, partly in free village communities, but for the most part in some degree of subordination either to church landlords or to the military aristocracy. Every freeman was obliged to equip himself with arms for service in the *fyrd* or militia, and upon his class had rested for over a hundred years very heavy responsibilities in the way of local police duties and of interpretation of local custom and national law against wrongdoers. That is, the freeman had both to join in the pursuit of cattle-rustlers and other criminals (hue and cry) and to perform scrupulously his parts in the determination of innocence or guilt and in an intricate system of fines and compensation which had been gradually built up as a substitute for lynch law and blood feud. The American frontier was to repeat this pattern in many ways six or seven hundred years later. Below the freeman were the semifree and slaves. Above him were the aristocracy of church and kingdom who had some conceptions of life in terms of a larger unit than shire or village. They formed the Witenagemot or royal council of magnates, and individuals among them made what they could of the regional authority which accompanied the offices of archbishop, bishop, abbot, or earl or ealdorman of a shire or group of shires.

The incoming Norman aristocracy had been born and bred to feudalism, a form of administration which had sprung up all over Europe when stable central government had been destroyed by the wars and barbarian migrations which had been going on since the fourth century. Practically it amounted to the breakdown of government into local units, each under a kind of contractual relationship, called vassalage, with a higher suzerain, or feudal lord. Naturally, much depended upon the relative strengths of vassals and suzerains or lords. Duke William, for instance, was formally the vassal of the king of France for the fief of Normandy, but actually that mattered little. Indeed, his real problem was to maintain his suzerainty over his own vassals, who held the subdivisions of Normandy as smaller fiefs under him.

The problem was simpler in England because William had the whole conquest at his disposal. He kept a good deal of it for himself and divided the rest up by confirmation of Anglo-Saxon grants, or by new grants to his followers or to Anglo-Saxon magnates who came to terms with him. In return for these concessions he demanded direct allegiance to himself as well as specific amounts of military service by fully equipped knights. Soon after the Conquest he brought his whole design into view by conducting the national census of population and property which we know as the Domesday Book. The king's vassals repeated the feudal procedure with the huge estates which they had received from him, so that in theory at least there was an orderly pyramid of men reaching down from the Conqueror to the lower clergy and to the actual workers on the soil or in the trading towns and cities. King William took some wise precautions: he alone could concede the right to build a castle, he retained the Anglo-Saxon militia, and he endeavored to keep alive, particularly in the shire unit, the police and court duties of all freemen. He meant to be king in fact and that meant that he must forearm himself against his immediate vassals, the so-called tenants-in-chief.

This was a military conquest, not an inundation of one people by another. A few thousand Normans ruled the mass of the English and made French the language of the upper classes. The folk continued to speak their varieties of English, but they had to carry their poetic literature in their memories. For the most part they became the silent actors on the stage, biding their time until their sheer weight of numbers and what they could learn from their conquerors should bring them into their own. The island melting pot had a great variety of material to work on during the two or three centuries which were to elapse before the re-emergence of the English.

CHAPTER III

The Lion and the Unicorn
1087–1485

"The Lion and the Unicorn were fighting for the Crown." The old nursery rhyme about the British coat of arms might well be taken as a symbolic summary of the contests which went on from the end of the eleventh century to the end of the fifteenth between the monarchy and the feudal nobility or between factions of king makers. Kings did their best to raise themselves above their tenants-in-chief, the "peers of the realm," while the magnates fought and conspired to keep the kingdom and the crown within their power.

Some monarchs, of course, men of the type of William I, Henry I, Henry II, and Edward I, were able to keep on top through sheer ability, but others, like John, or Edward II, or Richard II, or Henry VI, were incapable of grasping the essential nature of their office or of using its prestige and advantages in a beneficial way. Because of these ups and downs in the quality of the monarchs, what happened to them individually is less important than what happened to the office of kingship and to the other institutions related to it which Englishmen came to value and preserve, independently of the kind of king they had, because they worked agreeably to English temper and circumstances and because they made life a more orderly and predictable affair.

THE BRITISH ISLES

Liam Dunne

SHETLAND ISLANDS

ORKNEY ISLANDS

John o'Groats

THE HEBRIDES

The Minch

MORAY FIRTH

Inverness

SKYE

KYLE OF LOCHALSH

Aberdeen

Glencoe

SCOTLAND

MULL

Dundee

FIRTH OF LORNE

St Andrews

FIRTH OF FORTH

ISLAY

Glasgow

Edinburgh

FIRTH OF CLYDE

New Lanark

NORTH SEA

Londonderry

NORTHERN IRELAND

Belfast

SOLWAY FIRTH

Newcastle

Sligo

Galway

Drogheda

ISLE OF MAN

York

IRISH SEA

Liverpool

Leeds

Hull

EIRE

BOYNE R.

Dublin

ANGLESEY I.

Manchester

Sheffield

Grimsby

Limerick

Channel

ENGLAND

Cork

Aberystwyth

WALES

Birmingham

Norwich

Cape Clear

St. George's

Rugby

Stratford-on-Avon

Cambridge

BRISTOL CHANNEL

Swansea

Cardiff

COTSWOLD HILLS

Bristol

Oxford

RIVER THAMES

Lands End

Glastonbury

Bath

Windsor

LONDON

Canterbury

SCILLY ISLANDS

Southampton

Portsmouth

SUSSEX

Dover

Dunkirk

ATLANTIC OCEAN

Plymouth

Beachy Head

Strait of Dover

GRIS NEZ

Calais

Gravelines

FLANDERS

Boulogne

PICARDY

Scale of miles

0   50   100   150   200

ENGLISH CHANNEL

CHANNEL ISLANDS

Alderney

Guernsey

Jersey

La Hogue

Cherbourg

RIVER SEINE

Havre

Dieppe

NORMANDY

FRANCE

N

W   E

S

Thanks to the trial-and-error in the ways of government and self-government which went on between 1066 and 1485, the world owes much to the people of an inconspicuous island off the coast of Europe. They worked out stubbornly and persistently, and ultimately gave to other parts of the earth, two remarkable English products—the Common Law, which gradually shapes itself to the changes which take place in society and to which even kings must bow, and parliamentary institutions, which allow the politically self-conscious members of a society to determine the character and policy of their own government.

Between 1066 and 1189, three great kings, William I, Henry I, and Henry II, made up for the backslidings of two bad ones, William II and Stephen, by imposing an ingenious structure of royal government upon Norman and Anglo-Saxon alike. They did much of this by force, but they gave their apparatus lasting powers by one clever device—the expansion of royal justice, at the expense of feudal justice, and in alliance with the old Anglo-Saxon system of freemen's responsibilities. That is to say, the king built up his feudal court, Curia Regis, and then cut under the feudal courts of his vassals by sending out his officials to revive the Anglo-Saxon courts of hundred and of shire as local royal courts, at first for royal business and then for the business of his subjects. Royal justice had the enormous advantage of being final; royal judges not only conciliated opinion by paying great respect to local customary law, but as they accumulated and recorded their decisions they digested all kinds of law into one, the national Common Law; and, perhaps most important of all, through the use of local accusing and trial juries they forcibly associated the substantial elements of the people in their work. An American historian has called the process "self-government

at the King's command." Gradually and almost impercepti-
bly, royal justice became national justice, at first only in
the criminal field, but finally in the civil field as well.

The great problem of national administration, then as
now, was revenue. The courts were counted upon to furnish a good deal from fines, fees, and confiscations, the royal
estates provided a very substantial portion, and various conventions of the feudal contract between king and vassals
brought in still more. When unexpected demands arose,
or the royal treasury ran dry, a good king was expected to
put this problem up to his tenants-in-chief at a regular or
special meeting of Curia Regis. A bad king simply used
his authority to abuse the operations of royal justice or to
extort revenue from individuals in breach of his feudal or
other contractual relationships with them.

After Henry II's death, his son Richard, the Lion-Heart,
a glamorous crusader who spent most of his reign away from
home at great cost to his subjects, began to exploit unjustly
the immense powers which he had inherited and turned
over to able administrators. His brother John, who succeeded him, went much farther. Between 1199 and 1215,
this evil, rapacious tyrant perpetrated such intolerable
cruelties and excesses that he provoked a rebellion which
even his remarkable military abilities could not quell.

His victorious opponents met with him at Runnymede,
near Windsor, early in the morning of Monday, June 15th,
1215, and by nightfall he had accepted their terms and
attached the imprint of his great seal to the label of their
list of demands. By Friday all the details had been settled
and several copies of Magna Carta, the Great Charter, were
sealed for distribution in the kingdom. A king had been
forced to admit that even he was below "the law" and to
agree to a very precise definition of the contractual rela-

tionships between him and his vassals. He promised not to levy most kinds of extraordinary feudal taxation without consulting the entire military caste and the great ecclesiastics, and not to resort to arbitrary imprisonment or punishment. He made some other promises to the church and to town governments. Thus the Charter was a most important step in broadening the base of English government. It did not, however, improve directly or to any great extent the political status of the common man. Only since the seventeenth century have the English-speaking peoples greatly broadened the application of its principles.

Already, however, the central government was trying to enlist the co-operation of classes other than the tenants-in-chief, particularly for the supply of taxes. Kings like Richard and John sold town charters which authorized self-government in return for annual payments, and John invited various shires to choose knights, that is, feudal sub-vassals, who should consult with him and his council about the needs of the day. During the reign of Henry III (1216–72), who was far too much impressed by papal pressure and other foreign influences to be a good king for England, the sheer force of circumstances upon the king and his opponents brought about a loose and precarious merger for regulation of the English central government. This structure, along with practically all the other institutional and legal apparatus of the time, was overhauled and made crisper and more efficient by Henry III's hard-bitten son, Edward I (1272–1307).

It was called "the King in his Council in Parliament," that is, the monarch, his personal advisers and professional administrators, and the tenants-in-chief (laymen and churchmen) meeting for a parley or consultation. At first the representatives of the lesser clergy, the townsmen, and the knights of the shire were only occasionally summoned as supernumeraries, but they represented so much wealth that during the fourteenth century the representative burgesses and knights came to form a regular part of Parliament, the House of Commons. During the same century the principle was established that taxes could be levied, old law stated, and new law pronounced only by the joint action of King, Lords, and Commons. Two kings, Edward II and Richard II, were deposed and killed in the process of reaching those conclusions. England had become a constitutional, that is a limited, monarchy by 1399. In fact it was so limited that it soon degenerated into a series of faction fights which almost wrecked England before Henry Tudor won the crown by battle in 1485.

The wealth which was evidenced by the growth and broadening of central government indicated that the Normans had made it more possible for the people of England to develop their island's productivity. It is true that there was a great deal of civil war and war abroad, but this was carried on, with relatively little effect on the general population, by the feudal military class and by increasing numbers of mercenaries or of freemen (yeomen) who joined companies which were chiefly paid out of loot, as, for instance, during the Hundred Years' War with France (1337–1453). Moreover, the Northmen had always known how to combine trading with warfare wherever they went, so that not only did London and other commercial centers profit by the Norman Conquest, but the rising commercial classes made a good thing out of equipping and supplying armies and out of exploiting the markets in France and Flanders which victorious English armies opened to them. English capital resources were swelled by loot and by the ransoms which captured French nobles extracted from their subordinates and transferred across the Channel.

English production rested upon the broad foundation of village agriculture, most of which was meshed into the feudal military and political structure by the manorial system. The last is a modern term of convenience, for manorialism was notably unsystematic, but its more common characteristics can be put together to illustrate it in outline. Everywhere local peculiarities were reflected in variations of the scheme. The idealized manorial unit, however, would be a village of humble cottages, each with a small garden and orchard plot, grouped under two superior edifices—the parish church and the manorial hall. There might also be a mill and, more rarely, an inn. The priest supervised morals, conducted Christian education, and dispensed the sacraments of salvation. The lord of the manor or his steward or overseer, with the assistance of a manorial court or assembly to which all owed attendance, ran the manor, primarily for self-subsistence, but also, if possible, for surpluses which could be taken to the trading towns.

The village lands lay around it like a single farm, divided into plowland, meadow, and waste. Cattle pastured on the common; pigs foraged the woods; sheep ranged upland pastures. The whole plowland was divided into three great fields, so that one was always fallow in a three-year rotation of wheat or rye and beans or barley, and each field was divided into narrow strips, several of which, on land of varying quality, made up an individual holding. A substantial proportion belonged to the lord "in demesne," and was worked for him by the serfs, or villeins, as part of their payment to him for their own much smaller holdings. Originally these serfs were bound to their lands, but as time went on the more enterprising bought their freedom. Manorial managers were increasingly willing to agree to this as they came to realize the advantages in efficient work of hiring free laborers. Three disastrous visitations of bubonic plague (the Black Death) in the fourteenth century also accelerated the end of serfdom, for it killed off a third or a half of the population, leaving the surviving land cultivators in a stronger bargaining position.[1]

Probably the best land managers of this medieval period were the monks and higher clergy, who accumulated large permanent estates from the gifts of the faithful, and who were in touch with new ideas and improved farming as conducted by other ecclesiastical farm managers on the Continent. In particular, churchmen seem to have taken the lead in sheep farming, and wool, along with hides and leather, rapidly became the most important English surplus for export. For centuries English wool went to the skilled weavers of Flanders. Only towards the end of the fourteenth century did the English begin to develop their own wool manufacture round the skills and machinery of imported Flemish workers.

As production increased and surpluses became available, England became a land of towns and cities [2] as well as of villages. Here merchants maintained shops and markets, and craftsmen displayed to passers-by the articles which they and their journeymen and apprentices had made on the premises. England needed sellers of grain and malt, brewers and bakers, tailors and leatherworkers, candle makers and metalworkers. At regular intervals great fairs were held at stated places, where foreigners exchanged what

[1] The Peasants' Revolt of 1381, although treacherously and savagely repressed, was an incident in the same process.

[2] Usually the sites of cathedrals, but also towns created cities by royal charters.

they had brought for what they wanted to take away. London and certain other great ports became places for the assembly of export commodities such as wool, leather, dried fish, lead, tin, cloth, and ironware. At first, foreign traders established trading posts in England, much as the English were later to do in India and China, but by the latter part of the fifteenth century it was clear that the process was about to be reversed. The rich island was almost ready to invade the markets of the world.

By the fourteenth century, particularly during the reign of Edward III (1327–77), English society was a well-ordered structure. At the top was the glowing, luxurious court, where the king and his son, the Black Prince, tried to live up to the idealized standards of chivalry which had been elaborately set forth during the past two or three centuries by the poets and courtiers of other courts, notably in the south of France. They revised and elaborated the legend of King Arthur and the Knights of the Round Table, developed a cult around an Arthurian shrine at Glastonbury Abbey, and founded the Knightly Order of the Garter, with its smug motto, "Honi soit qui mal y pense." Much of this was empty nonsense, as some notorious behavior of the English during the Hundred Years' War attests, and at its best chivalry was a code of generous behavior which the nobility did not think of extending to the lower classes, but Edward's court was probably the most notable of its day in Europe. The truth was, however, that chivalry as a high aspiration, accompanied by long and rigorous education and self-discipline, had passed its peak of usefulness at least a century before.

Below the magnates of the realm were the smaller landowners, that is, the squires or gentry, many of whom became knights and some of whom climbed the social ladder still higher by prowess, wealth, or marriage. They shouldered a good deal of responsibility for local government as justices of the peace, churchwardens, members of the shire (or county) court, and members of the House of Commons. They raised companies of the best archers in Europe for the wars and were the natural leaders of the yeomen, that is, the freemen who held land worth at least forty shillings a year and who elected the knights of the shire and served on grand and petty juries. Below the yeomen were the lesser freemen and the serfs who were breaking the bonds of servitude.

The church, to which all gave allegiance, provided parallels to these gradations of society. The two archbishops, of whom Canterbury was the superior, approached the king himself in prestige, and the bishops and the abbots of the greater monasteries were truly magnates of the realm. The church had had separate courts, both for its own members and its own business and for certain lay cases involving matrimony, oaths, and wills, since the time of William the Conqueror. Its landed estates and other revenues were enormous. All over England were magnificent monasteries, and the begging friars of the orders of St. Francis and St. Dominic had also acquired imposing houses here and there. Generally speaking, however, after centuries of unquestioned leadership, their increased wealth and the scandalous career of the papacy during the fourteenth century had made the upper clergy and the members of the orders a very worldly lot. The admiration of a keen observer like the poet Chaucer went out only to the lowly, but usually devoted, parish clergy, whom economic circumstances kept very close to the level of the lives of their humble flocks.

Towns and townsmen varied considerably. London, as one of the great cities of Europe, with a population of forty to fifty thousand persons, was the resort of merchants and bankers from the principal commercial centers of Christendom. Its great gilds, or societies, of merchants and craftsmen were rich, assured, and powerful, not only in terms of London's affairs, but of England's. Thanks to the representation of the burgesses in Parliament, the Londoners were beginning to outgrow the old provincialism which had made citizens of other English towns "foreigners," and to glimpse the desirability of a national commercial policy. As it was, they had to admit already that certain ports, like Bristol, Southampton, and Hull, enjoyed special advantages, and that certain towns, like the rich wool centers in the Cotswolds, the ironworking towns of Kent and Sussex, the mining centers of Cornwall, and the cloth towns of Yorkshire, must be conceded substantial weight in the general economic scheme of things. Shipowners and merchant adventurers who traded with Europe from the Baltic to the Mediterranean also contributed their share towards broadening horizons.

This urban aristocracy was much looked down upon by the landed nobility and gentry, for whom only the profession of arms conferred honor, and who shared the church's distrust of those who bought at one price and sold at a higher. This convention of scorn for those "in trade" persisted almost down to our own time and was largely responsible for a phenomenon which, in rather meaningless forms, is quite as perceptible today around the great cities of the United States as in Europe. The rich English townsman hastened to buy himself a country estate and to learn the accomplishments of a country gentleman. He himself might not be admitted to "County" society, but with luck his children might, and there was always the chance of entry into the sacred ranks by marriages which could replenish impoverished, if aristocratic, treasuries. This process was made easier in England than elsewhere in Europe because English hereditary titles descended only through the eldest son, leaving an ever-growing group of gentry whose social standing was good, but who had to make their own places in the world without benefit of noble title or of the entailed (inalienable) family estate which went to support it.

Below the "masters," or aristocracy, of the towns and cities were all sorts and conditions of men. Within the craft guilds were the youngsters who worked out their years of apprenticeship with varying fortunes and the journeymen who had gone beyond this and who hoped for the success which would make them masters. In the same way the master merchants were poised on a pyramid of aspirants for their positions. And, as always, the shelter and the opportunities which cities offer attracted hosts of the ambitious and the unfortunate. Some of these were fugitives from serfdom hoping to take advantage of a fairly common convention by which they could break free through establishing acknowledged residence within a chartered town for a year and a day. Others were riff-raff—horse holders, street sweepers, and beggars, who preferred the risks and excitement of vagabondish town life to an ordered place and responsibilities in rural society.

About 1340 there was born to a vintner, or wine dealer, of London, a son who was named Geoffrey Chaucer and who summed up better than any other individual what had been happening to England during the past three centuries. This young Londoner first made his mark as a page in the household of Edward III's third son, went to the wars in France, and, when taken prisoner about 1360, had part of his ransom paid by the King, who took him into his own service. He married a knight's daughter whose sister married another of Edward III's sons. He served Richard II and Henry IV before he died in 1400 and was buried in the south transept of Westminster Abbey, where his tomb became the nucleus of what we now know as Poet's Corner.

Although Chaucer made his mark on his day as a diplomat abroad and an official at home, he made his place in history by writing unsurpassable poetry in English. After three centuries of submergence below the Latin of the church and the Norman-French of the court, the old language of the conquered, purged and simplified by the elimination of many of its Teutonic declensions and inflections, and enriched by borrowings from the languages of the upper classes, burst through into general usage. In Chaucer it found a master so winning, humorous, compassionate, and witty that his well-told stories in verse still enchant readers who have to use a glossary in order to understand many of his words, and an intricate, unfamiliar system of pronunciation in order to recapture his lilting rhythms. In spite of the fact that his poetic models (and much of his material) were Latin, French, and Italian, he gave whatever he wrote an unmistakably English character. *The Canterbury Tales* bring the whole of fourteenth-century England to life as Chaucer conducts the reader in a company of thirty-one travelers from Harry Bailey's Tabard Inn at Southwark [3] along the Pilgrims' Road to the shrine of St. Thomas à Becket at Canterbury. We know our England, our pilgrims, and their countrymen by the time the four-day journey and the pilgrims' story-telling competition are done. It is fitting that William Caxton, the first great English printer, who set up for himself at Westminster in 1476, and who yielded to no man in the intensity of his English patriotism, applied the new invention at once to securing for Chaucer's poetry

[3] A borough of London south of the Thames.

the broad audience which his genius and popularity commanded.

Chaucer was not the only great English intellectual of the Middle Ages. The universities which sprang up, at Oxford towards the end of the twelfth century and at Cambridge early in the thirteenth, were parts of an international structure of learning whose common language was Latin and whose teachers and students were all clerics of the universal church. They moved about from place to place with great freedom, so that a great scholar might teach all his life in a foreign country. England, Scotland, and Ireland furnished perhaps somewhat more than their share of these scholars. Ireland intellectually refertilized much of Europe in the seventh and eighth centuries. York provided Charlemagne with his great educator, Alcuin. And in the gallery of Europeans who laid the foundations of modern learning, the British contingent, as represented by Grossetête, Ockham, Roger Bacon, Duns Scotus, and Robert of Gloucester, was an outstanding one.

Universities and churches, rather than castles and palaces, embodied the high artistic achievements of the times. The grim old Norman style of architecture could be lightened a little in buildings which did not have to function as fortresses, but it was suddenly swept into disrepute by the daring grace of the Gothic style which crossed over from France in the reign of Henry II and was used in rebuilding the choir of Canterbury Cathedral. The new mode, with its immense pointed windows and lofty open spaces, was a marvelous adventure as it pitted the close calculations of the architect against the forces of gravity and of wind and weather. Walls and towers were pierced and raised until they seemed mere lattices, which were capable of supporting high-pitched roofs only by grace of strong buttresses leaning against, or even flying out from, their pillarlike substantial sections. Stained glass, wall paintings, mosaics, ecclesiastical utensils and vestments, and carved stone or wood gave endless opportunities for the remarkable decorative skills which had been native in England since earliest times. The cathedrals, abbeys, churches, and colleges which an ever wealthier England built in great numbers between 1200 and 1500 were primarily receptacles for religious aspiration, but also for a love of beauty which we can still recognize in spite of the destruction wrought by time, or perhaps more ruthlessly, by the Puritans' passion for making all things plain. Today it requires great knowledge and imagination to clothe the restrained beauty of even a beloved national shrine like Westminster Abbey with the glow and color which Henry III gave it in the thirteenth century. In days when few could read, church walls and church windows told the drama of Heaven and Hell in vivid pictures.[4]

Singularly enough, many of these imposing religious buildings were built during times when thoughtful and influential Englishmen were strongly out of sympathy with the Roman Catholic church. Down to the twelfth century the church, by right of its leadership in nearly every human aspiration, had enjoyed an almost unquestioned pre-eminence and universal loyalty. The Conqueror had given the church in England its own courts, and when Henry II tried to make criminal churchmen subject to royal justice he failed, because four of his knights had thought to please him by murdering Thomas à Becket, the Archbishop of Canterbury, who was opposing him. During the thirteenth century powerful Popes exploited their power by asserting

---

[4] In addition, between 1300 and 1420, remarkable cycles of scriptural plays were composed for presentation at religious and civic festivals.

a feudal, that is, political suzerainty over England and her kings and by requiring a feudal tribute from them. This ill-judged entry into high politics in England and elsewhere in Europe provoked a widespread adverse reaction. If the church insisted upon becoming worldly, it must expect to be judged by worldly standards. Many intellectual leaders in Europe, Dante for instance, tried to persuade the church to withdraw into the religious sphere, but in vain. Inevitably, therefore, during the fourteenth and fifteenth centuries the church fell into grave disrepute. The papal office became a football for rival factions who thought of it in political and economic terms. The monastic and mendicant orders forgot their spiritual ideals. The once universal church was rent by worldliness, schisms, and heresies. Thoughtful Catholics, laymen and clerics alike, were in despair because the directors of their church seemed incapable of undertaking its reform.

English kings, from the end of the thirteenth century onwards, took the line of shaking off papal political and financial controls, but this was not enough.[5] Laymen like Chaucer and churchmen like William Langland spoke for educated groups who rightly but vainly demanded that the church recall its proper function of religious leadership instead of falling behind. The consequence was that since protest in England could evoke no reforming response, part of it became a heresy known as Lollardry. John Wycliffe, a Yorkshireman who taught at Oxford, boldly declared that the wicked Popes derived their powers from the Roman Caesars, not from Christ or St. Peter, a novel doctrine which was popular at first with the politicians. They grew alarmed, however, when he went on to deny the central Catholic

[5] The capture and domination of the papacy by France was particularly objectionable.

doctrine of transubstantiation in the Mass; the Archbishop of Canterbury and the King drove Wycliffe and his followers out of Oxford; and it was from a country rectory that he subsequently launched his English translation of the Bible and the "poor priests" who went about condemning many Catholic practices and preaching in English a direct relationship between man and God without the mediation of a priest. Once the movement was cut off from its educational base at Oxford, church and state combined to stamp it out, using the approved medieval methods of inquisition and burning at the stake. Lollardry was driven underground early in the fifteenth century, not to emerge again until the break-up and reform of the Catholic church a hundred years later.

In retrospect, the fifteenth century in England, at least until Henry Tudor of the House of Lancaster became Henry VII in 1485, seems like a fruitless time. The Hundred Years' War against France, although marked by another amazing victory for English bowmen at Agincourt in 1415, ended in 1453 with the loss of all French territory except Calais after Joan of Arc had aroused a sense of nationality among hitherto fatally divided Frenchmen. In England itself the weakness and subsequent insanity of Henry VI plunged the country into wars among the magnates [6] which lasted, with interruptions, from 1453 to 1471, and from 1483 to 1485. Wars abroad and at home had bred such contempt for orderly ways that sheer force had debauched the functions of kingship, Parliament, and the law. Members of the productive classes—farmers, craftsmen, and traders—never knew when their enterprises would be wrecked by some accident of war or by the un-

---

[6] Wars of the Roses, between backers of the princely houses of York (white rose) and Lancaster (red rose).

thinking greed of men who had grown callous through generations of violence.

Yet, if order could somehow be restored, England had since 1066 built up elements of strength which could be welded together to make the most remarkable national state in Europe. The Tudors were to capitalize these advantages most shrewdly between 1485 and 1603. They did not create them. It seems worth while, therefore, to size up the opportunities which they might seize and develop.

To begin with, the English had learned some of the advantages of living on an island. In Henry II's time, England had been merely one part of his enormous Angevin empire, most of which was on the Continent, but Richard and John had managed to lose most of these Continental possessions. The Anglo-Norman magnates who expelled the French forces which came over during John's last struggles to fish in troubled English waters were wittingly or unwittingly defending what was henceforth to be their homeland, for they now had to choose between an English king and a French one. Henceforth, for almost six hundred years, the islanders had little to fear from their neighbors. Henry II had already planted English authority in the Irish "Pale" round Dublin. Edward I (1272–1307) conquered Wales and overawed Scotland, although both countries remained capable of giving a good deal of trouble at times. English military adventures in France and elsewhere in Europe, which went on intermittently during the thirteenth, fourteenth, and fifteenth centuries, provoked no French invasions of England in response.

In fact, England enjoyed the immeasurable advantage over other young national states in Europe of having no really dangerous land frontiers and of requiring very little in the way of naval protection in order to reinforce her watery defenses. The sheer saving of national energies which this made, as soon as the English realized the futility of trying to hold pieces of the Continent, gave them decided superiority in subsequent international competition. Insularity, once made real, as it was in John's reign, was the nursing mother of nationality.

This relationship was made clear during the reign of Henry III, John's son. That weak monarch made a fool of himself many times through his inability to say "No" to the covetousness of the Pope or of his wife's relatives from southern France. By so doing he provoked in the English upper classes a hatred of foreigners which their less nationalistic fathers could hardly have understood. Henry's son, Edward I, expelled the Jews from England in 1290 and frankly used antiforeign sentiments for his own purposes. Edward I's own son lost his throne and his life partly because of his taste for foreign favorites, and the next king, Edward III, began the Hundred Years' War against France. English military successes at the expense of a divided France produced a cockiness which found expression in soldiers' songs on the subject of how many Frenchmen it took to equal one Englishman.

Englishmen not only had a land and a sense of nationality of their own, but they had regained a common language.[7] It was true that the Midlands dialect used by Chaucer and Langland was a sort of compromise between the dialects of north and south, and that local variations in speech which made it difficult for a peasant from Yorkshire to understand one from Somerset were to persist for hundreds of years, but Middle English was more generally understandable than Latin or Norman French. It became the language of

[7] "The King's English," or East Midland language, used at the universities and the court.

the law courts after 1362. Wycliffe put the Bible into this English and his poor priests used it in preaching their simple evangelical faith. The fifteenth century was the heyday of popular ballads, many of which crossed the Atlantic two centuries later and have survived in the southern Appalachians to our own times. And when printing came in about 1475, words began to assume fixed forms and to be increasingly simplified.

Finally, England had wealth and the means of making more. Foreign visitors invariably commented upon how well the English lived. A marked increase in population after 1450 meant that men were marrying younger and doing better for themselves and for their children. Beautiful buildings, growing towns, and larger fleets of merchant shipping were concrete evidence that, in spite of wars, England was accumulating capital. Agriculture was flourishing. The English cloth trade was so important to Europe that whatever town in the Low Countries handled it left its competitors far behind. Bristol on the west coast was the midway point in a sea-borne exchange of southern products from the Azores and Portugal for codfish which were taken as far away as Iceland. These and many other activities made it obvious that while feudalism was committing suicide in the Wars of the Roses, farmers, craftsmen, and merchants were perfecting their methods of production.

Naturally, these producers wanted peace. They saw no merit in wars on the Continent and they yearned for a strong hand to curb the antics of the magnates. They were far less interested in the exact legitimacies of inheritance of the throne than in the possibility of finding an occupant for it who would amount to something. They had had a glimpse of what they wanted between 1471 and 1483 when the Yorkist Edward IV had ruled in peace and in a kind of jovial understanding with the mercantile community in London. The subsequent troubles of 1483–85 were depressing, but if the Lancastrian victor at the battle of Bosworth Field in 1485 should prove himself a masterful, wise king, even his Welsh name might be forgiven him. The rising "middle" classes, the money-minded venturers in industry, commerce, and finance, were ready to welcome and to support a strong, if understanding, monarch who could impose order on a land which was bursting with constructive energies.

CHAPTER IV

Power and Glory
1485–1603

In 1513 a Florentine diplomat and military organizer named Niccolò Machiavelli was imprisoned, tortured, released, and banished to his farm by the Medici family, who had just recaptured his city, from which they had been expelled in 1494. While they had been in exile, Machiavelli, in the course of his duties, had been studying with a cold and calculating intelligence the savage conflicts among the papacy, the south Germans, the Spaniards, and the French, whose commonest battleground was northern Italy. Now, having decided that the whole medieval European structure was corrupt and crumbling into ruins, Machiavelli set himself the task of distilling from his experiences and from his remarkable knowledge of Roman history a formula for absolute despotism which should be based upon a science of politics and should be unhampered by ethical considerations. He hoped that some Italian would read the propositions which he set down in his textbook of autocracy, *The Prince,* and use them to unite divided Italy into a single state capable of protecting itself by a national army.

Machiavelli's book was so brilliantly clear and consistent that his name has been synonymous with despotism ever since. Its central creed was the identity of the ruler with the state. Anything which strengthened or weakened either had the same effect on the other. The prince must proceed towards his goal, that is, greater and greater power, without yielding to any irrelevant considerations such as humane or religious feelings. He must know human nature so thoroughly as to be able to manipulate it coldly for his own ends. On these foundations, Machiavelli laid down his laws of politics and even prescribed the precautions necessary to diminish or ward off accidental misfortune. Many a despot since has tried to put his ideas into practice. Several have succeeded for a considerable time. Yet all of these systems have eventually crashed because of the considerations which Machiavelli excluded. Men are religious, they esteem humane actions, they cherish ethical standards, and they refuse to remain for long mere wax in the hands of the politicians.

The point to be made here is that Machiavelli was the mirror of his times. All over Europe, emperors, kings, and princes, wrestling with the same disintegration of medieval standards, were thrown back on sheer practicality and expediency in order to maintain and increase their power. War was one instrument, marriage another, and assassination, direct or by legal pretense, still another. Religion and religious organizations must be subordinated to politics. In fact, rulers and would-be rulers claimed for themselves a new morality, the right to decide for or against any action whatever on grounds of "reason of state." Few, if any of them, went all the way with Machiavelli, for they compromised with decent human characteristics more than he would have thought safe. In particular, the Tudor monarchs in England between 1485 and 1603 practiced every Machiavellian technique, but their success in maintaining themselves until their line ran out seems good evidence that they possessed broader and more judicious imagination than the great political writer of their time. For one thing, they exercised almost absolute power without a standing army and without a large professional bureaucracy.

Henry VII, the founder of the line, was a secretive, wily, avaricious builder of despotism. His own marriage united the Lancastrian and Yorkist factions, his sons Arthur and Henry, in succession (1501, 1509), married the Spanish princess Catherine, and his daughters became queens of Scotland and France. His victory in the Wars of the Roses gave him practical and legal advantages over his recent opponents which he exercised artfully so as to weaken them and strengthen himself without provoking rebellion beyond his power to quell. In this way he not only collected so much revenue as to be almost independent of Parliament, but he endowed the monarchy with the greatest royal treasure in Christendom.

One of his shrewdest policies was to use middle-class men, whom he could make and break at will, as his principal administrators instead of feudal magnates who claimed office by hereditary right. Thus he secured the absolute obedience of able men and still further diminished the influence of the nobility. Finally, he won the sober support of the mercantile community by the ever-broadening order which he imposed on England, by allowing foreign monarchs to pay him not to wage war, and by advantageous trade agreements with the Low Countries and Italian trading towns. He broadened English control over Wales and Ireland.

All this was intentionally unspectacular, but even before Henry VII died in 1509 it was obvious that young Henry, heir to the throne since Prince Arthur's death in 1502, was going to cut a wide, flamboyant swath in Europe. He was eighteen at the time of his accession and already a spoiled, if remarkably gifted, young man. He was handsome, an

outstanding athlete, and enough of a scholar to delight
Erasmus, Europe's prince of scholars. He showed at once a
harsh, calculating temper, which was to grow more callous
with the years, by executing two of his father's administrators whose extortions had filled the treasury but made them
unpopular. He then proceeded to burn his fingers in the
course of some sixteen years of spectacular but unprofitable
interventions in Continental politics which exhausted his
treasury. At the end of it, all that he had to show on the
right side of the ledger was a colorful court, a crushing victory over the Scots, and some useful beginnings of a navy.
His gravest disappointment, however, was that of the several children which he had by his wife Catherine only one,
the Princess Mary, survived.

Henry VIII's determination to found a dynasty in the
male line led him to make six marriages, somewhat to the
amusement of other European princes.[1] What made the
matter exceptionally serious in Henry VIII's case was that,
in the course of terminating his first marriage, he involved
himself in a contest with the papacy which ended in the
separation of the Church of England from Rome.

Yet Henry's marital troubles were the occasion, not the
cause, of the break with Roman authority. Henry was an
ardent Catholic who had received from the Pope the title
of "Defender of the Faith" because of a pamphlet which he
wrote against Luther's Protestantism. Furthermore, he incorporated the principal articles of the Roman Catholic
faith in English statute law so that his rejection of papal
authority should not encourage Protestant doctrine. The

[1] Marriage with Catherine, mother of Mary, annulled in 1533; Anne
Boleyn, mother of Elizabeth, beheaded for traitorous adultery in 1536;
Jane Seymour, died in 1537 giving birth to a frail son, Edward; Anne of
Cleves, divorced in 1540; Catherine Howard, beheaded for traitorous adultery in 1542; Jane Parr, survived the King.

King of England separated his country's church from Rome
because he, like many of his contemporaries in Europe, refused to admit that papal authority was superior to his own.
The papacy had descended to such depths of worldliness
and avarice that its would-be defenders were helpless. As in
Wycliffe's day, the outraged feelings of critics like Luther,
Zwingli, Calvin, and many others, grew until they found
vent in repudiation of Catholic doctrine. When churchmen
were worldly, there seemed no reason why they should continue to enjoy possession of the properties with which they
had been endowed for spiritual purposes. On Machiavellian principles a sovereign prince might increase both his
power and his wealth by breaking with Rome, putting himself at the head of his state church, and confiscating as much
of its property as seemed desirable. That is what the rebellious princes of Germany did after Luther's defiance, and
Henry VIII followed suit.

The best evidence that the break-up of the unity of Christendom in the sixteenth century was largely a political affair is that it was dealt with by kings and princes in political
terms. After a generation of warfare between Protestants
and Catholics in the Germanies, the princes, in their loose
association which was known as the Holy Roman Empire,
found their peace formula in the phrase of 1555, *cujus regio
ejus religio,* that is, each ruler was to dictate the religion of
his subjects. Henry VIII had persuaded the English Parliament to co-operate with him in that very policy during the
'thirties and, although his church was severed from Rome,
King and Parliament made it illegal not to observe Roman
Catholic doctrine. If a man like Sir Thomas More insisted
on denying that the King was "the only Supreme Head in
earth of the Church of England," he lost his head, but mean-

while others, who could be convicted of the Lollard or Protestant heresy, were burned at the stake.

No one dreamed of tolerating a variety of religions in
those days, for no one believed that a state could survive
such disunity. The masses were docile, indeed it is impossible to escape the conclusion that the European peoples of
the sixteenth century either had very little deep religious
conviction or very little capacity for defending it. It was
not until the seventeenth century that the extension of
printing, preaching, and education meant that hosts of
lowly men like John Bunyan, the tinsmith, found in their
religion the passionate motivation for their lives.

Consider what happened in England between the death
of Henry VIII in 1547 and the accession of Elizabeth in
1558. Edward VI was a sickly boy of nine whose advisers,
or regents, again working with Parliament, converted the
Catholic English church into a Protestant one. They
adroitly turned on and off the flow of Lutheran and Zwing-
lian propaganda from the Continent, enforced the use of
the Bible and the Book of Common Prayer in English, eliminated Catholic rites, and finally laid down Protestant doctrine by statute.

Yet when Edward died in 1553, the Catholic princess
Mary succeeded to the throne in spite of a plot to make the
Protestant Lady Jane Grey [2] queen. Mary quickly got Parliament to repeal both the Edwardian and the Henrician
reformations of the church, thus making it a part of the
Roman church once more. She would even have dared to do
what a good many German princes were at that moment
fearfully avoiding, that is, restore to the church its confis-
cated property, had not her Spanish husband, Philip II,

[2] Granddaughter of Henry VII's younger daughter, Mary Tudor.

and other Catholic advisers warned her not to try it. Mary reigned five years and burned heretics at least as vigorously as her father had done, but when she died in 1558 and Anne Boleyn's daughter Elizabeth succeeded her, the new Queen and Parliament swung England completely back into the Protestant ranks again. It was a docile or a nonreligious English people that had accepted four major changes in religion in about twenty-five years.

Queen Elizabeth, who reigned from 1558 to 1603, could have taught Machiavelli a good deal, for she was a superlative artist in the chief technique of politics, that is, the management of men, and her imagination as to their motives of behavior was broader than the Italian's. She also had the rare gift of estimating accurately the materials with which she had to work and of being able to decide on the rare occasions when it was necessary to risk all on a single throw. Her life had depended on her wits almost since babyhood, for her mother, Anne Boleyn, had lost her head and Elizabeth her legitimacy before the child was three years old, and England had been full of conspiracies concerning the succession ever since. By courage, intelligence, and cunning she had survived the ups and downs of 1547 to 1558 without mortgaging her future in any substantial way. This hard-bitten, well-educated, somewhat coarse-grained woman came to the throne her own mistress, and free to make whatever decisions in religion, politics, and matrimony seemed best calculated to enhance England's strength and her own.

The outlook was distinctly forbidding, and certain far-reaching decisions had to be made at once, the chief of these being the matter of religion. After years of skillful resistance by a long succession of political Popes to all manner of public demand for ecclesiastical reform, the Roman

Catholic church was about to set its house in order under
Pius IV. A church council, which had been evaded,
thwarted, and pushed about from pillar to post since before Luther first split the church, was finally to be allowed
to get to work on the spiritual reconquest of Christendom.

Elizabeth seems to have been personally indifferent to
religion, but there were two strong inducements for keeping England Catholic. In the first place, it would avoid a
lot of troublesome adjustments and rearrangement, and, in
the second, it would provide less excuse for hostility from
Catholic France and Spain. Philip II, of Spain and the
Netherlands, lately joint sovereign of England with Queen
Mary, had the broadest realms and the richest colonies
known, but he thought enough of England to want to
marry Elizabeth in order to retain control. He was the self-
elected right arm of the Catholic church and would certainly not marry a heretic.

In spite of these considerations, Elizabeth and her advisers decided to play a lone hand, not only in religion but
in politics generally. The Queen's frequent boast that she
was "mere English" was a fit slogan for English nationalism
as it was asserted during her reign. The church became
Protestant and national. Philip was kept dangling as long
as possible, as were other suitors, none of whom won the
Queen. Spain was thrown on the defensive through English
aid given to her rebellious Protestant Dutch subjects.
France was similarly embarrassed by assistance to the Protestant Huguenots and to a Protestant faction which
quickly threw off French control of Scotland. Within a
year or two, Elizabeth and her England had shaken free of
outside influence and embarked on an exhilarating, if risky,
course alone.

Elizabethan England faced and defeated three great challenges or, perhaps better, three challenges in one. The first was the existence of Mary Stuart, great-granddaughter of Henry VII, Queen of Scotland from her birth in 1542, and Queen of France for a few months in 1560. To all Catholics she, not Elizabeth, was the legitimate Queen of England. This winsome, able, and energetic widow arrived in Scotland in 1561, after twelve years at the corrupt court of France, to find John Knox's Presbyterians in control. Thanks partly to her Catholicism and partly to her unfortunate second and third marriages, she was forced to flee from Scotland to England in 1568, thus becoming the captive of Elizabeth and leaving her infant son, James VI of Scotland, in the hands of Scotland's Protestant controllers.

The second challenge was that of the papacy. The reforming Council of Trent finished its work in December, 1563, a reformed Jesuit order at once began to launch its militant missionary offensives, and Pope Pius V excommunicated Elizabeth in 1570, declaring that she was a usurper of the throne and absolving her subjects from allegiance to her. England was to be rewon at all costs, and now all Catholic hopes and conspiracies centered on Mary Stuart. The Catholic north of England rose in 1569–70 and was savagely repressed. The Duke of Norfolk, leading nobleman of England, was executed in 1572 for conspiracy with the papacy and Spain in behalf of Mary. Elizabeth turned loose her piratical seamen on the commerce and colonies of Spain, rooted out and killed as many as possible of the courageous Jesuit missionaries, and redoubled her aid to the Dutch rebels and to the Huguenots whose leaders were so treacherously massacred in Paris in 1572. Her harassed advisers reported plot after plot to assassinate her and to enthrone Mary. Finally, after seventeen years of a tension which drove ministers, Parliament, and Protestant patriots almost frantic, Elizabeth authorized the execution of Mary in 1587.

Now slow-moving Philip of Spain decided to carry out the papal decree of deposition for his own benefit, thus uniting the menaces to Elizabethan England. In Spain he assembled the most overpowering fleet in European history, the "Invincible Armada," and in the Low Countries his military commander gathered thousands of Spanish veterans for embarkation and conquest. Late in July, 1588, one hundred and thirty ships, bearing thirty thousand men, came bowling up the Channel driven by a wind which forced the English to tow out their vessels in order to meet them. Two hundred light, fast English ships, standing off at cannon range, poured metal into the floating castles of Spain as they proceeded towards the armies waiting in the Netherlands. When the Spaniards sought shelter at Calais, the English drove them out by fire ships to meet their guns again and also to meet a gale which first swept them along the Flemish coast for another battle and then changed to drive them out into the North Sea. Only sixty ships and about ten thousand men got back to Spain by rounding Scotland, leaving wrecks and a few survivors on the rocky coasts of Scotland and Ireland. The English struck two medals to celebrate their island's deliverance through sea power, but they gave God credit for the victory. "He blew," the saying went, "and they were scattered."

It took some time for Englishmen and other Europeans to realize what had happened. It seemed incredible that in thirty years the small Island Kingdom had fought free from, and effectively repelled, the combined assaults of the papacy and Spain. Actually the Anglo-Spanish War went on intermittently for another fifteen years; but now, with Spain on the defensive, English aid prevented Philip from exterminating the Protestant Dutch Republic and from eating away the natural strength of France by dividing that nation. Spain was obviously in decline and the Dutch, the French, and the English were in the ascendant. The stream of history entered upon a new course during the summer of 1588.

Yet with Mary Stuart dead and the unmarried Elizabeth in her mid-fifties, the House of Tudor had run its course so far as the main line was concerned. The common assumption was that the throne would pass to James VI of Scotland, whose descent in one way or another united the best hereditary claims originating in the family of Henry VII. England would not be endangered by this succession of a foreign prince, indeed she would be strengthened, for the greater kingdom would eclipse the lesser and the danger of Scotland's serving as a base for attack on England would be diminished.

In fact, the British Isles were in a fair way to be considered united under one authority. Henry VIII had completed his Welsh father's work by incorporating Wales in his kingdom and it was now both Protestant and represented in Parliament. Ireland had been kept weak and divided by playing off the clan leaders against each other and by favoring now one and now another of the great Anglo-Irish families. The various stages of the Anglican Reformation were imposed on Ireland as a matter of course with little apparent effect on the Celtic-speaking Irish save the disappearance of their old monastic centers of education. Confiscation of Irish church lands and the landed establishment of the alien Anglican church introduced a new batch of English exploiters, colonizers of a land which was neglected and outside the main stream of European development.

Suddenly, however, English rule and religion were challenged by the revitalized Church of Rome. The Jesuits and other missionaries took advantage of England's combination of neglect and abuse of Ireland by making a truly penetrating reconversion of the Irish to Catholicism. Henceforth this unfortunate people had at least one vital thing in common, and passionate devotion to an unrecognized church became for centuries to come almost synonymous with passionate hatred of English rule. There were three Irish revolts during Elizabeth's reign and they cost the English treasury as much as all the Queen's other military and naval expenditures combined. The rebellions were savage affairs on both sides, marked by foreign intervention, treachery, assassination, and massacre. The end of them was the first complete English military conquest of Ireland, and soon after Elizabeth's death this was followed by the expulsion of the native population from large areas in the north (Ulster) for the benefit of colonies of Protestant English and Scots. The tragedy of modern Ireland had its real beginnings during the expansive Elizabethan age.

There had been other attempts at colonization during Elizabeth's reign, notably in Newfoundland and "Virginia," [3] but they had failed. The reason was that throughout the Tudor period England was painfully engaged in accumulating the capital in experience, ships, equipment, and hard cash which must be acquired before colonization could succeed. Portugal and Spain, by their mastery of the new art of ocean navigation under the schooling of alert Italians during the latter part of the fifteenth century, had respectively won a monopoly of the route round Africa to the East Indies and a monopoly of the Americas before Henry VIII ascended the throne; in fact, the Pope had divided the whole non-Christian world beyond Europe be-

[3] Actually on the coast of present-day North Carolina.

tween them. Portugal's immense profits from Eastern trade
and Spain's takings of bullion from Mexico and Peru left
England (and all other European competitors) far behind
in the new race for national wealth.

With no East Indies or Americas to draw upon for addi-
tions to her liquid wealth, England had to grow rich in
other ways. As we have seen, she had for sale surpluses of
tin, lead, iron ware, wool, and woolen cloth. She caught
fish and cured them for foreign markets. She looted other
nations during wars. By excluding foreigners from her
maritime carrying trade, she gradually built up a mercantile marine both for her own services and for the income
from carrying the trade of others. In brief, the once despised
island outpost of Europe now capitalized her position
astride the new commerce which had been opened up by
ocean navigation and struck out for world leadership in
sea power. The traditional skills of her shipbuilders and
sailors had free play. The English navy became one of fighting ships, sea-borne batteries instead of floating barracks.
The new ships were so fast and maneuverable under sail
that they could avoid coming directly to grips with their
more ponderous opponents. Merchant ships followed suit
so closely that in time of crisis they merged easily with the
navy.

All these things England did during the sixteenth century, but, compared to Portugal and Spain, her own enrich-
ment was slow. Since the southern routes to India and
China belonged to others, English mariners made prodigi-
ous efforts to get there through the arctic seas north of
Russia and the Americas. They failed, of course, but the
Newfoundland and New England fisheries were some
consolation for these enterprises. Since English merchants
wanted tropical products and had chiefly heavy woolens to

offer in exchange, they had to operate for the most part through foreign middlemen, whether Portuguese and Spanish, or the operators of the great commercial exchanges in the Low Countries and the Levant, or the inhabitants of the Baltic countries and Russia. Some English merchants made astounding overland journeys from arctic Russia and the Levant to Persia and India, turning over successions of goods all the way there and back, with desperate risks and small profits, for the sake of the knowledge which the Portuguese sought to deny them. "Our chiefe desire," wrote Hakluyt, "is to find out ample vent of our wollen cloth."

A quicker, if slightly more precarious, road to riches was to break into the Portuguese or Spanish monopolies in some way. John Hawkins, for instance, built upon his father's earlier ventures to Portuguese Africa and Brazil, and upon his own knowledge of French buccaneering exploits in the West Indies after 1521, a most ingenious plan which he put into operation before Philip II broke with England. In the winter of 1562–63, with a good deal of Spanish connivance in Europe and the West Indies, he bought or captured about four hundred negro slaves on the Portuguese west coast of Africa, took them to Hispaniola (Haiti) and, in spite of the regulations against foreign traders, sold them for pearls, hides, sugar, and a little gold. Owing to some unavoidable miscalculations, this voyage was only moderately successful, but a second, in which Elizabeth herself was a shareholder, earned some 60 per cent. The third voyage of 1567–69 ended in disaster at Vera Cruz, Mexico. Here Hawkins and a Spanish fleet came to blows and henceforth scheming had to be displaced by outright piracy, privateering, and finally war.

The English never scored such spectacularly profitable individual successes as did the French and the Dutch against

Spain, in the Atlantic and the Caribbean, along the Spanish Main, and on the Isthmus of Panama, but they did better for themselves in the long run by their persistence. Drake's astounding harvest of bullion for ballast of his little ship, the *Golden Hind,* taken from the Pacific coast towns which he surprised in 1578–79, made every adventurous lad in the West Country yearn for his chance at such fame and profits. Thanks to the fluid society which had emerged from the decay of feudalism in the fourteenth century, the new sea venturers were drawn freely from gentry, middle class, and lower class, on naval vessels, privateers, and merchantmen alike. After 1500, England's principal "career open to talents" was life on the seas which surrounded her. After Spain gobbled up Portugal in 1580, Englishmen even began to think of emulating the Dutch by going out to India and the Spice Islands by sea and breaking into the Far Eastern preserve.

One had only to travel about England to realize that the country was rich and getting richer. The old half-timbered rubble houses and halls were giving way to large and elaborate buildings of brick and stone which were adorned inside and out with a wealth of taste and fancy. Gardens and parks were the objects of pride and competition. Wood carvers, silversmiths, and goldsmiths satisfied eager demands for the kind of display which a hundred years earlier had been pretty much confined to princely palaces or to the wealthiest homes in northern Italy and the Low Countries. Clothing and jewelry became gorgeous—an ambitious courtier might wear a whole manor on his back. At court, in London, at nobles' country seats, and in the mansions of the gentry, all was glow and color—the pride and ostentation of a society on the rise.

It was fitting that this exhilarating, exuberant age pro-

duced in Shakespeare the greatest genius of the English
tongue. This country-loving son of a small burgess of Strat-
ford found his way to London about 1584 when he was only
twenty. By 1592 he had risen sufficiently in the world of the
theater to excite a jealous attack from an older hand at the
game.[4] From then on, recognition of his pre-eminence grew
rapidly, for no sensible man could deny that as poet, drama-
tist, and revealer of all man's thoughts, feelings, and im-
pulses, he was unsurpassed. It was not that he had no competitors, for this was the age of Marlowe, Jonson, Greene,
Spenser, and Francis Bacon as well, but Shakespeare saw
so much, so deeply, and so clearly, and put his perceptions
in such unforgettable language that he stood quite alone,
as he does today. He began his career with five patriotic
plays which, in the years just after the Armada, tellingly
reminded Englishmen of how much better off they were
under the Tudors than in the days of feudal faction. He
may, indeed, have been a paid propagandist for national
unity in those perilous times. But with *Venus and Adonis*
and *The Comedy of Errors* of 1593, he was off on his own
course of high comedy and deep tragedy, wherever his fancy
or his philosophy led him.

He wrote some of the most beautiful songs we know, for
Elizabethan England formed the crest of a century and a
half when the English were the most musical people in
Europe. Tudor church music, Catholic and Protestant, was
so good that it has been systematically collected and repub-
lished in our time. Henry VIII was merely one among many
who wrote words and music for their love songs. Elizabeth
prided herself on her skill on the virginals—the instrumental predecessor of spinet and harpsichord. And everyone

---

4 Robert Greene, who referred to him as "an upstart Crow" who "is in
his owne conceit the onely Shake-scene in a countrie."

sang. The most popular entertainment of all classes was part singing, with or without instrumental accompaniment, of madrigals and other musical forms whose intricacy and range sometimes tax the capacities of expert singers today. There was plenty of grinding misery, uncurbed violence, and sudden death in Elizabeth's England, but with it went an effervescent zest in life which betokened a people who, consciously and unconsciously, were finding expression for their highest powers in every kind of action.

Elizabethan misery deserves a word, if only because it evoked the first nationally comprehensive scheme of social legislation of modern times. Probably the basic cause of the rapid economic changes which dislodged and damaged so many persons in the sixteenth and seventeenth centuries was the sudden, enormous, and sustained influx of gold and silver from the Americas. In England prices doubled and tripled and did so at a time when modern business practices, particularly the habit of looking at all ways of making a living in terms of capital investment and interest, were upsetting agriculture, industry, commerce, and finance. The confiscation of the monastic and other Catholic charities diminished, although it did not destroy, the old apparatus for dealing with the unemployed and helpless.

"Hark, hark, the dogs do bark, the beggars are coming to town." The old rhyme signalizes the sudden, appalling problem of vagabondage with which authority had to deal throughout the sixteenth century. At first the response was half charitable, half savage. Gradually, however, the whole complex of related problems of apprenticeship, wages, the unemployed employables ("sturdy beggars"), the sick, the aged, and the infants, was comprehended in some great statutes of Elizabeth's reign. The burden of administration fell upon the unpaid local nobility and gentry, whether as justices of the peace, those Tudor maids-of-all-work, or as churchwardens. They bound out apprentices, set wage scales, raised funds for hospitals, and built workhouses. The parish was the basis. To it in terms of birthplace were directed the able-bodied and the impotent poor, the former to earn their keep in the workhouses, the latter to be looked after in hospitals and poorhouses. Rough and ready as the structure was, it served England with but slight modifications until 1834 and it was the model for much that still exists in other parts of the English-speaking world.

Viewed as a whole, Tudor rule was certainly despotic, but it was successful because sovereigns like Henry VII, Henry VIII, and Elizabeth succeeded in identifying themselves and their actions with the good of the state and the people. It seems strange to speak of such ruthless killers as the Tudors as benevolent despots, but their enthusiastic subjects thought them so, and through the device of Parliament the politically conscious elements of the nation believed with some justice that they shared actively in the government of England. The Tudors on the whole used Parliament somewhat sparingly. They had enough sense to allow themselves to be guided, and even occasionally thwarted, by Parliament at those times when its will was unmistakable. They needed its approval of their policies in the form of statute law, and in emergencies they needed it for extra taxation. Above all, it was the great symbol of their respect for traditional, constitutional ways. Actually royal initiative and ultimate powers were exercised through the Council and through the increasingly vigorous conciliar courts, but the impression was conveyed that these were interim and emergency powers, while the normal exercise of government went on through Parliament and the common-law courts.

After the papal excommunication of 1570 and the breach with Spain, the Tudor system of conciliar government began to run into difficulties. Parliament demanded a much more arbitrary policy towards Rome and Spain than the wily Queen judged desirable. The purchasing power of royal revenues fell year by year, and Parliament refused to tax the nation enough to pay for what it expected the administration to do. The Queen and her advisers tried all sorts of expedients, such as the sale of monopolies, but since these were rapidly and inevitably revealed to be indirect taxes, Parliament demanded their abolition. Most ominous of all in the Queen's eyes was the clear reflection in Parliament of a Protestantism which was almost as contemptuous of Anglican uniformity and episcopal authority as the national church was of Rome. Elizabeth, like her father, was just as ready to execute a Protestant nonconformist as a Catholic one and she did so to the end of her reign, but the radical left wing had courage and it found brave men to speak for it in the House of Commons.

All in all, then, whenever Queen and Parliament met between 1570 and 1603, there was every prospect of a first-class struggle. Stubborn men lost their liberty, their property, and even their heads for their opposition, but the struggles went on, ever more skillfully on both sides. The Queen lectured the Commons and the Commons demanded freedom of speech. When the Queen's ministers or ultra-loyal members demanded more than the Commons thought reasonable, "all the house hemmed and laughed and talked." Yet as the reign drew towards its close, and men looked back on what had been achieved, they could not help but be proud of the painted old lady in her gorgeous raiment who so gallantly personified England's new power

and glory. They continued to fight her to the brink of disaster. She continued to thwart them as far as she dared.

In 1601, after a long and bitter contest over monopolies,
the aged Queen called her full Parliament before her for a
speech to them which she no doubt thought might be her
last. To everyone's delight, instead of hectoring and abus-
ing her opponents, she addressed the Commons with great
eloquence and real affection, concluding:

> There will never queen sit in my seat with more zeal to my coun-
> try, care to my subjects, and that will sooner with willingness yield
> and venture her life for your good and safety than myself. And though
> you have had and may have many princes more mighty and wise
> sitting in this seat, yet you never had or shall have any that will be
> more careful and loving. . . . And I pray you, Mr. Comptroller,
> Mr. Secretary, and you of my council, that, before these gentlemen
> depart into their countries, you bring them all to kiss my hand.

It was a fitting curtain for the unforgettable drama of her
reign.

CHAPTER V

Civil Liberties and Colonies
1603-1689

IN MANY ways, the seventeenth century was the most remarkable hundred years in the development of western
civilization. All kinds of ferments which had begun to break
down orthodox views and traditional authorities during the
fifteenth and sixteenth centuries now showed widespread
effects. Men who had believed that their earth was the center of the universe came to realize that it was merely one of
many celestial bodies in a sun-centered system whose laws
of motion could be mathematically demonstrated. New instruments, like telescope and microscope, and new mathematical aids, like analytical geometry, logarithms, and the
calculus, invited men to examine and chart nature for themselves instead of relying upon scriptural revelation. Men
who thought that European civilization was the pinnacle of
human achievement began to borrow eagerly from other
civilizations in India, China, and the Americas. In Europe
itself the old aspirations towards a single church and a
single state gave way to many churches and many states.
Within the national states, despotic rule and religious uniformity were successfully challenged by republicanism and
religious toleration. The hold of Portugal and Spain on
commerce with the overseas world was broken by France,

Holland, and England. Europe was in turmoil, and all manner of modern, revolutionary ideas boiled up here and there, forcing societies to compromise with them or submerge them. Everywhere authority was in conflict with freedom.

In Britain this medley of forces had such amazingly free play that it would be difficult to think of many aspects of life in the modern English-speaking world whose broad origins could not be found during this turbulent century. The catalogue would be a long one, yet an enlightened Englishman of 1700, looking back towards 1600, would have been likely to single out three great achievements. These would be: the political revolution by which sovereignty passed from the Crown to the propertied classes; the commercial and colonial contests in which England began definitely to move ahead of Holland and France; and the rapid scientific advance which was crowned by Sir Isaac Newton's demonstration that his law of gravity could explain the operation of the whole universe in relatively simple mechanical terms.

When the great contest between the Men of Property and the Crown began in 1603, few persons realized how fundamental it was going to be. James I was a very learned, but only moderately wise, man who had put together a theory which he supposed would make it easier for him to carry on the paternalistic despotism of the Tudors. In it he demonstrated to his own satisfaction (and bolstered up with endless scriptural texts and illustrations from history) that kings were divinely appointed and maintained, that they were accountable for their actions only to God, and that their subjects must obey them, leaving it to God to determine what sort of rule they received. Parliament was to serve as an advisory collaborator, and the common-law courts were to handle ordinary judicial business, but in high policy and emergencies the King would act independently of both through the Council and the conciliar courts which the Tudors had set up. The whole scheme was closely knit and appealed strongly to men of authoritarian temper, but it needed an artist like Elizabeth to make it work, and no Stuart monarch except Charles II had her capacity for knowing when it was expedient to sacrifice principle and to give way to stubborn opposition.

James's chief opponents were the propertied classes—a small group of noble landlords, a much larger group of landed gentry, or squires, and a growing number of men engaged in commerce, industry, and finance. In a good many ways they were not much wiser than he was; indeed they and their like caused a lot of unnecessary trouble for about a century by refusing to tax themselves heavily enough to pay for the services which they demanded from the national administration. The great trouble on both sides was that men had become money-minded at a time when the value of money was declining rapidly because of bullion imports from the Americas and when a small number of men who had learned how to manipulate money and instruments of credit were provoking violent booms and depressions.

The Men of Property insisted that the King should "live of his own," that is, keep within his ordinary income from his estates and traditional revenues, except in emergency, when Parliament and, in Parliament, the House of Commons would vote what it thought necessary by way of taxation. Further to protect their position, they looked to the common-law courts as defenders of their lives, liberties, and property against any arbitrary action of King, Council, and conciliar courts. In these circumstances it is easy to understand why Sir Edward Coke, the outstanding common-law judge of the time, was James I's chief opponent, both as a judge until he was dismissed, and as the astute guide of the Parliament thereafter.

It is understandable, too, that the Men of Property countered James's theory of monarchy by appealing to the past history of Parliament and the common law. Learned antiquarians like Coke and his friend John Selden resurrected ancient records going back four hundred years or more. Among other things they located Magna Carta, which had been so thoroughly forgotten that Shakespeare never mentioned it in his *King John,* and they eagerly transformed some clauses of that contract between a feudal king and his tenants-in-chief into a set of useful constitutional principles which should sharply restrict a seventeenth-century king in his relations with a whole people.

Running across the lines of this contest was the fatal complication of religious differences, no longer merely between Protestant and Catholic, but much more among various kinds of Protestants. Thanks to the firm establishment by the Tudors of the state church, and to the conflicts with the papacy and Philip II which had made patriotism almost synonymous with anti-Catholicism, there was little likelihood of any welcome to the ancient faith and church. If there had been, it would have been destroyed by the unsuccessful Guy Fawkes conspiracy of the Catholics to blow up King, Lords, and Commons when Parliament assembled on November 5, 1605.[1]

The chief religious issue now was the one which had so

[1] The hard core of English anti-Catholicism, then and later, stemmed from the papal power to absolve subjects from their allegiance, as exemplified by the excommunication of Elizabeth. From then on, fear and nationalism united to reject this foreign authority which might be used to override English sovereignty.

alarmed Elizabeth during the last years of her reign, that is, the growing Puritan movement which demanded very simple church rites and austerity in personal life. Since the obstacles to these ends were the hierarchy of the church (the episcopacy) and the Court of High Commission which enforced its orders, the Puritans hoped to achieve their ends either by substituting the Presbyterian system of ecclesiastical authority which was built up from below, or by abolishing the episcopacy and letting each congregation follow its own bent. Like every other monarch in Christendom, James insisted upon a uniform state church, and he was very well satisfied with what he found. "No Bishop, no King," he said, and he castigated all nonconformists with his remark, "Jesuits are but Puritan-Papists." His opponents, Catholic and Protestant, borrowed each other's arguments for removal of this barrier to their ambitions, although all of them save the Congregationalists were just as firmly committed to imposing their own brands of intolerance as the Stuart King himself.

Thanks partly to the authoritarian tradition established by the Tudors, and partly to the many divisions among his opponents, James I stumbled through his reign without an overt rebellion and died in his bed in 1625. He had pursued a thoroughly unpopular foreign policy by peace with Spain and by failure to aid the Protestants in the Thirty Years' War which was ravaging Germany; he had dissolved three Parliaments because they had opposed him concerning taxation and concerning their own freedom of speech; he had scandalized the Puritans by the extravagance and moral laxity of his court; and his only constructive contribution during the raging religious excitement of the day had been his authorization of what proved to be a magnificent English version of the Bible. Yet Englishmen did not know quite what to do with a stubborn king and they were too little of one mind for any majority to agree on a substitute.

Charles I, who succeeded his father in 1625, was, if anything, more stubborn and was certainly either less wise or less capable of understanding the rapid changes which were going on around him. He threw away his original advantage of personal popularity by marrying a Catholic French princess [2] and by clinging to his father's arrogant and stupid favorite, Buckingham. When Parliament refused to back him generously with taxes, he collected additional revenue by forced loans and other irregular devices. He made the mistake of consenting to the Petition of Right of 1628 which provided against these procedures and against the means for their enforcement and then going back on his word next year. For the following ten years he did without Parliament, collecting various forms of revenue by arbitrary authority, backed by subservient judges and courts. His opponents were forced to bide their time.

Their chance came when the Presbyterian Scots, rebelling against Charles's determination to impose the Anglican church upon them, invaded England.[3] The King, unable to find the money to pay an army of his own, was finally forced to put up with the famous Long Parliament. Brilliantly led by John Pym, and containing many such victims of arbitrary imprisonment as John Hampden, this Parliament maneuvered the King into stripping himself of the apparatus of despotism. He lost his two principal aids, the

[2] His mother, Anne of Denmark, had been converted to Catholicism.

[3] Presbyterianism contributed greatly to contemporary republican ideas because its congregations, both individually, and collectively in their presbyteries and assemblies, were organized and governed along republican lines.

Earl of Strafford and Archbishop Laud, the conciliar courts were abolished, and non-Parliamentary taxation was declared illegal.

Charles was waiting for religion to divide his opponents, but by the time that it did, in 1641, matters had gone too far to be settled otherwise than by war. After seven years of confused contest, power passed, not to Parliament, but to the resolute, professional army which it had created. Its leaders, having discovered unmistakably that Charles was an unconscionable liar and was prepared to use Irish, French, or Scottish aid for the re-establishment of absolute monarchy and religious uniformity, decided after much prayer and heart-searching that his continued existence was certain to prolong civil conflict. In 1649, Oliver Cromwell and the army officers purged Parliament, used the remnant, or "Rump," to justify the trial and execution of the King, and set about imposing order on the British Isles.

Cromwell and his associates were chiefly Congregationalists, believers in religious toleration for all save Catholics, Unitarians, and atheists. They allowed the Jews to re-enter England after three hundred and fifty years of exclusion. They were genuinely anxious to set up a republic with a parliamentary system of government. Yet they were up against the fact that since 1640 or 1641 there had not been any realizable majority in England. The Cavaliers (royalists) included not only moderates but also Anglican and Presbyterian extremists. The Roundheads were an impossible mixture of moderate Anglicans and a dozen other religious sects, most of them intolerant. And since civil war has a way of releasing all kinds of opinion, their camp included oligarchical republicans, outright democrats, socialists, communists, and such strange groups as the Fifth Monarchy Men, who believed that Jesus Christ's kingdom on earth was about to be set up. The result was that although Cromwell tried again and again to set up a parliamentary system, even resorting for once in English history to a written constitution, his concern for order and property always made him alarmed by the critical spirit in these assemblies, which he successively dismissed in favor of military rule.

When Cromwell died in 1658, it was apparent that England had utterly failed to agree upon some republican substitute for the former monarchy. Once this conviction took hold, it was inevitable that Charles II, heir to the throne, should be invited to return from the Continent. He came back in 1660 amid scenes of profound relief and rejoicing, pledged only to rule in collaboration with Parliament. He did not, he admitted, want "to commence his travels again." Although pleasure-loving in the extreme and more than willing to follow the pendulum swing away from Puritan austerity, he proved himself to be quite the cleverest politician in England by riding the waves of violent, revolutionary clashes of opinion until he died, practically an absolute monarch, in 1685.

The story of how Charles II divided and defeated his opponents is a fascinating but very complicated one, marked by a calamitous visitation of bubonic plague, the destruction of London by fire, a Dutch fleet in the Thames, panic fears of "the Popish Plot," private and judicial murder, and so on—in short, by times of such turbulence, mystery, and fear that Charles was able to convince the sober-minded that he alone stood between them and chaos.

In general, his success was based upon this growing conviction and upon two astute and cynical lines of policy. He held the whip hand over Parliament because he sold the control of English foreign policy to his cousin, Louis XIV of France, for enough money to make him relatively independent financially. And, although secretly a Catholic by conviction (and by profession on his deathbed), and originally determined to set up in England with Jesuit aid the same sort of despotism as Louis XIV and members of the Society of Jesus had devised at Versailles, Charles was clever enough to discover that a Catholic despotism was impossible in England and unprincipled enough to use authoritarian Anglicanism instead.[4]

James II, who inherited his brother's smoothly running despotism in 1685, clumsily destroyed the whole mechanism, almost entirely because he was a devoted Catholic. Like his father and unlike his brother, he set fidelity to his church first, and he was stupid enough to believe that he could succeed politically where Charles II had failed.

Quite simply, he set out to make England Catholic again, and, just as he did so, English anti-Catholicism was intensified by the relentless persecution of the Protestant Huguenots in France and the flight of thousands of them for refuge in England. None the less James proceeded to dismiss Anglicans from all kinds of high office in church and state and army and to put Catholics in their places. The politically conscious elements of the nation began to draw together in angry, but almost helpless, opposition. They did not want another civil war and they might have put up with James and awaited the succession of his Protestant daughters, Mary and Anne, had not the Queen after fifteen childless years given birth to a son early in the summer of 1688.

The prospect of a Catholic dynasty was too much. The leaders of the nation invited William of Orange, Stadholder of Holland and husband of James's daughter Mary, to come in, expel James, and take over the government temporarily.

---

[4] Charles's opponents had cleverly appealed to anti-Catholic and anti-French sentiments by the slogan, "No Popery, no wooden shoes."

The officers of the army abandoned their King; the navy offered no resistance; Louis XIV, who might have aided, was campaigning on the upper Rhine; and the royal family fled. The "Glorious Revolution" of 1688 was, in fact, also the "Bloodless Revolution" so far as England was concerned. The Highland Scots rose, with temporary success, for their Stuart King, but their clan leaders soon consented to be paid for taking on the new allegiance.[5] When James, with French aid, attempted to use Ireland and its hapless people to regain his throne, William himself went across to defeat his father-in-law at the Battle of the Boyne. This third conquest of Catholic Ireland by Protestant England within a century engraved still more deeply the antipathies between the two island peoples and between the south and north within Ireland itself.

The new king struck as hard a bargain as he could with his new people, whose aid he wanted in the long duel with Louis XIV which he had been waging in behalf of Holland since 1672, but in spite of his determination and of his immense usefulness to his English hosts, the flight of James II had meant the end of old-style monarchy in England. Henceforth England was really a republic with representative government and with a hereditary, but closely curbed, executive. Various later monarchs were to endeavor to break their bonds and to rule as well as reign, but none was to succeed except briefly. Tradition and constitutional usage made it convenient to go on having a king, but sovereignty had passed for good to Parliament.

The bargain, or contract, was drawn up in the Declaration of Rights which William and Mary accepted and which, as the Bill of Rights, became law by Parliamentary

[5] A combination of delay, misunderstanding, and ruthlessness led to the massacre of the Macdonalds of Glencoe.

action.[6] Now instead of the King determining the religion of his subjects, the formula was reversed. Roman Catholics were forever excluded from the throne. The King was prohibited from interfering with the due process of law and levying taxes or maintaining an army without Parliamentary consent. The basic civil rights, as they had been laid down long ago to Charles I, were reaffirmed [7] and freely elected Parliaments were to meet frequently and enjoy freedom of speech.

Thus, after almost a century of wrestling with their rulers, the English had come to the point of resolving to rule themselves. Man, they decided, was not made for the state, but the state for man, and they planned to keep it so. They were not the first republic to be formed in Europe, for the Swiss and the Dutch had preceded them; but their experiment was to have profound effects all over the globe. Their so-called "constitutional monarchy" was not a democracy, although democratic principles had been explicitly formulated for the English-speaking peoples by the radicals and the Puritan Left in London and around the army campfires during the long Civil War. Neither had the English been able to get sufficiently far ahead of their times to commit themselves to complete freedom of religion, for like everyone else they still thought of religion in political terms. They were stubbornly anti-Catholic and, although by law they conceded free exercise of their religion to Protestant nonconformists, they confined the full rights of citizenship to members of the established church.

In brief, the Revolutionary settlement was a compromise. Three generations of civil disagreement had finally thrown

[6] The American Declaration of Independence followed its form quite closely.

[7] Among them Habeas Corpus, statutory recognition of which had been extracted from Charles II in 1679.

up a controlling majority of the politically conscious population. That group, composed of the propertied classes, had cast divine-right royalists, manhood-suffrage democrats, Roman Catholics, and non-Anglicans into political outer darkness. They formed an oligarchy—largely a landed oligarchy—and although they might quarrel among themselves and with their monarchs, they had taken a grip on sovereignty which they were not to loosen until 1832.

Their grand achievement was freedom from despotism, what they called "the liberty of the subject," or "the rights of Englishmen," and although this was confined to a small proportion of the population, yet it had loosed ideas in the world. John Locke wrote the theory of the Glorious Revolution after the fact—a crystal-clear enunciation of natural rights, government by consent of the governed, and sovereignty defensible only as long as it was exercised for the protection of the life, limb, and property of the governed. Less than a hundred years later, Thomas Jefferson was to be accused with some justice by his American critics of having echoed Locke's phrases in the Declaration of Independence.

Perhaps the best indication that things had shaken down into a workable compromise in England was that the Men of Property who had assumed sovereignty had at last come round to being willing to pay in taxes for governmental services. There were still to be many squabbles and a good deal of cheese-paring stinginess in the fiscal relations of King and Parliament, but now that Parliament was handling its own business when it administered the nation's business, it was ready to be reasonable about the bookkeeping. The royal debt became the national debt, and from a blend of English with Dutch, Jewish, and Scottish financial knowledge and experience a Bank of England emerged to serve as a bridge between public and private finance. A few astute men in Amsterdam, recently the financial center of Europe, decided to move to London, for there seemed to be a good chance that it was forging ahead towards world leadership.

The economic promise of the sixteenth century had been more than fulfilled in the seventeenth, in spite of civil wars and dissensions. Property had changed hands at an astounding rate, as it is likely to do in time of rapid economic change and war. Men who knew how to manage money took advantage, by way of loans and mortgages and other financial manipulations, of men who knew only how to manage land. Patriots turned over their liquid wealth to King or Parliament during the Civil War and it found its way into the hands of army contractors. The winners taxed the losers to maintain Cromwell's rule and managed in one way or another to acquire estates for themselves. Yet all the while England grew richer, more money was in circulation, and more people became expert in making money breed more money. In every rank of society some men became poorer, but England as a whole became richer in spite of political vicissitudes.

English trading companies were active in northern Europe, the Mediterranean and the Levant, and in India. The venture round Africa to the Persian Gulf and the Far East was a costly one, but the profits were so great that the English East India Company, like the Dutch East India Company, sent out armed ships which broke their way into the former Portuguese preserves along the west coast of Africa and on the Indian Ocean. The great obstacle to exploitation of these successes was that when Portugal's power was destroyed, the Dutch turned against the English and excluded them from the Spice Islands and Ceylon. This forced them into a most intricate series of trade exchanges in mainland India in order to convert English hardware and heavy woolens into spices and Eastern commodities. In fact, they found that their outbound ships had to take a good deal of hard money with them in order to bring full cargoes home, a practice which sorely troubled statesmen and politicians who were accustomed to measure a nation's strength by its supply of bullion. Gradually, however, it was brought home to them that the resale of Eastern goods to foreigners in Europe more than made up for the cash in the strongboxes outward bound round the Cape of Good Hope.

The Newfoundland fishery continued to flourish, and it was discovered that the banks off Nova Scotia and New England were rich enough to support settlement on the American continent, particularly if a fur trade could be developed on the side. As Captain John Smith said of the struggling early days, "Fish and Furres was then our Refuge." A colony established in 1607 farther south, in Virginia, almost expired until it found salvation in the cultivation of tobacco, a seductive narcotic which drove James I to an angry "Counter-Blaste," but which delighted so many less austere men that it put the colony permanently on its feet. This was achieved at the cost, however, of outright slavery for negroes and the half slavery of indentured white labor and transported convicts.

Bermuda was colonized in 1609 when some Virginia-bound ships were wrecked there, and from early in the seventeenth century there were numerous successful attempts to seize and hold from Spain advantageous island sites in the West Indies. After almost suicidal beginnings several of the American colonies had, fortunately, become self-sustaining by 1629, when Charles I, Strafford, and Archbishop Laud began their attempts at dictatorial rule of state and church. Consequently many a man who could not stand his political, religious, or economic lot at home cleared out for the free lands, the freer choice in religion, and the more republican commonwealths of America. American ministers of religion crossed and recrossed the Atlantic like real-estate promoters, and their books and pamphlets about the New World were marked by a good deal of poetic license.

In all of this early overseas enterprise the Protestant Dutch were England's chief rivals. They had more liquid capital, they built better ships (witness the number of Anglicized Dutch words like yacht, jib, boom, etc.), and they were probably better sailors. The Londoner Henry Hudson was working for them when he happened on the Hudson River and thus gave them New Amsterdam in New Netherland, the one great North American fur-trading center south of Canada. They massacred English interlopers in the Spice Islands, chased them off North Sea fishing grounds, and by 1650 they were in a fair way towards dominating the world's ocean-borne carrying trade.

But Charles I had just lost his head, and Oliver Cromwell was now in the saddle. During his nine years of ascendancy he not only conquered Ireland and Scotland and brought them into a legislative union with England and Wales, but he launched Robert Blake, a good soldier who became a naval genius, against his enemies on the seas. Blake fought the Royalist Prince Rupert, the Barbary pirates, the Dutch, the French, and the Spaniards, with startling success. All foreigners were excluded from the best parts of the English and English colonial carrying trade by the Cromwellian Navigation Act of 1651. New Amsterdam was marked down for capture in 1654, but when the Dutch made peace, Nova Scotia was taken from the French instead.[8] Jamaica

8 Charles II gave it back.

was captured from Spain in 1655. In brief, English naval and maritime power was re-established after its dangerous decay under the first two Stuarts.

The Restoration in 1660 failed to halt this revival. The English fought the Dutch with increasing success from 1652 to 1654 and from 1665 to 1667, but in 1668 the two countries formed an alliance against the imminent aggression of France. Thanks to Charles II's duplicity in putting England's foreign policy at the disposal of Louis XIV, that alliance was nullified for twenty years, during which the tremendous efforts of the Dutch to withstand Louis XIV's armies so held back Holland that England began to pass her in national wealth and strength. There was something symbolic in William III's migration from Amsterdam to London, for although Holland continued to grow more powerful, England's power grew faster still. The Thames instead of the Zuyder Zee became the site of the world's greatest port.

There had been a group of colonial expansionists at Charles II's court, men of influence who were awake to the great strides which had been taken in this field during the past two generations, and who had no compunctions about using the men and skills and knowledge which had been built up by their political opponents. It was this group which engineered the conquest of New Netherland [9] in 1664, thus closing the gap in the row of English colonies along the North American Atlantic coast; which built up a French-Canadian idea into the lucrative fur empire of the English Hudson's Bay Company; which founded the Carolinas; and which fostered the trans-Appalachian explorations from Virginia that carried Englishmen into the eastern Mississippi basin just as Frenchmen were about to

[9] Roughly comprising New York, New Jersey, and Delaware.

descend the great river from the Great Lakes. England had the makings of a commercial and colonial empire on a world-wide scale when Dutch William ascended the throne, and already the administrative apparatus for making that empire profitable had been tested and found good enough to place on the statute books.

Already it was clear that in North America the French were to be England's principal rivals. Before any Englishmen had planted themselves firmly on that great continent, the French had founded a settlement in Acadia (1604–05), and Quebec had been established the year after the Jamestown venture in Virginia (1607). Gradually, while the English solidly peopled the Atlantic coastal slopes and their river valleys from Massachusetts to South Carolina, the French spread out across the best lands of the Acadian bastion overlooking the North Atlantic fisheries and the Great Circle route to Europe, and launched their fur traders and missionaries into the mid-continent by way of the St. Lawrence and Ottawa rivers and the Great Lakes. When the English Hudson's Bay Company commenced its fur trading around the northern entry to the continent, the French began to raid and distress its establishments by daring overland journeys. When the New Yorkers began to drain furs from the interior by way of the Hudson, the men of the St. Lawrence systematically wooed the Iroquois middlemen to their side. The Canadians also pre-empted the great Mississippi waterway and its principal tributary, the Ohio, thus at the same time winning the mid-continental transportation routes to ocean waters at the Gulf of Mexico and setting up a potential barrier to the westward expansion of the English colonies.

North America, that is to say, was breeding conflicts, irrespective of Europe, before the seventeenth century ended.

With a whole continent to exploit, mere land was not greatly in question, but strategic positions for protecting profitable enterprise were another matter. River mouths on Hudson Bay; beaches and harbors close to the North Atlantic fisheries; rivers, lakes, portages, and passes which could be linked to draw furs to ocean waters from the interior —such areas were already in contest. And if in sheer imaginative daring and far-flung enterprise the French surpassed the English, the explanation, and in it the omen of the future, was not far to seek. The English had seized parts of North America which invited settled enterprise in agriculture, forestry, and commerce, whereas the French depended almost exclusively on fishing and the fur trade, nonsedentary enterprises which were quickly becoming secondary among the English colonists and which did not greatly encourage population growth. Enough immigrants poured into the English colonies of their own wills and by their own efforts to exceed by far the state-fostered peopling of New France. Already the English North Americans greatly outnumbered the French, and whenever the final reckoning should come, the disparity was sure to be overpowering.

Curiously enough, there was little reflection of the English imperial temper in the best literature of the day; in fact, there never has been except for Ralegh and Kipling. The wits and dramatists wrote amusing, bawdy plays about the dissolute court circles and the money-makers in the cities and their beautiful, susceptible wives; an occasional poet colored his stanzas with strange foreign names and vague references to enterprise overseas. But England itself and God's plans for "His Englishmen" were the themes of the century's literary spokesman, John Milton. This "God-gifted organ voice of England" was the bridge between the all-embracing, adventurous humanism of Shakespeare and the sober austerity of Puritanism. Milton had come racing back from Italy, his earliest spiritual home, to plunge into the conflicts against Charles I and Laud. During the Inter-regnum, he served Cromwell as an official and penned the most magnificent political and religious pamphlets in the English tongue.[10] Perhaps owing to the blindness which had come upon him in 1652, he was not persecuted after the Restoration, so that he was able to write the Puritan epic, *Paradise Lost,* and thus attain the station in literature to which he had consciously dedicated himself in his youth, before his country plunged into revolution.

Yet, although Milton was England's second greatest poet, he was almost unknown outside the British Isles, whereas John Locke was eagerly discussed abroad. Locke's fame came from his lucid, and to many minds conclusive, revelations of the principles or laws of human nature and understanding and of a system of natural rights upon which almost mathematically rational systems of society and politics might be reared. Milton once said that when God had some particularly important revelation to make he made it to "His Englishmen," and the intellectual leaders of Europe might have agreed in the case of Locke.

Still greater was their admiration for Isaac Newton. This self-taught genius seemed to have inherited all of the progress in mathematics, astronomy, and experimental science which had been made in the grand succession of Copernicus, Kepler, Galileo, and Descartes. From about his twentieth year he began to display profound insights into all manner of mathematical, astronomical, and physical problems which came to his attention. These insights carried him to

10 Notably his *Areopagitica,* the classic assertion of freedom of expression. "Give me the liberty to know, to utter, and to argue freely, according to conscience, above all liberties."

the enunciation of physical and mathematical principles and practices which experiment verified and which scientists and mathematicians have employed ever since.

What gave Newton his greatest fame was his discovery, probably in his twenty-fourth or twenty-fifth year, of the law of gravity. He was so diffident about this and so occupied with other things, that it was not until 1685 and 1686, when he was forty-three years old, that he was induced to bring together and publish his great discoveries as *Philosophiae Naturalis Principia Mathematica*. That book gave coherence to the entire sun-centered universe for the first time since Copernicus had argued for it. Newton's principles and Newton's mathematics transformed the great mystery into a smoothly working, predictable machine. To Newton's generation it seemed that God was at last revealing himself to man in the beautiful, simple principles of the natural universe.

It had been a wonderful century. In many fields Englishmen had aimed at human freedom and had won through to substantial success or the promise of it at moderate cost in human suffering. One or another had applied systematic doubt to the traditional, established ways in religion, politics, psychology, philosophy, and natural science. They had substituted experiment for acceptance of authority. They had put together their findings to form the foundation principles for new ways which were rooted in their empirical convictions.

The Protestant national church had won the support of a majority of the people, but the sectarian minorities were allowed to worship as they willed, thus signalizing the separation of church and state for which Locke argued in his *Letter on Toleration*. Divine-right monarchy had been superseded by the republicanism of a sovereign representative

Parliament which held the King, its executive, to a closely defined contract. After endless argument as to whether men were by nature good or evil, Locke had won approval by asserting that they began their lives with natures like blank slates upon which experience alone engraved their personalities. In philosophy inductive reason based upon measurement of material things had taken the place of deduction from general principles. "How" had pushed in ahead of "why." In natural science, using the new mathematical and instrumental aids and the experimental method, William Gilbert had opened the approach to magnetism and electricity, William Harvey had discovered the circulation of the blood, Robert Boyle and Robert Hooke had demonstrated many of the properties of gases, and other members of the so-called "Invisible College" of 1645 which was the nucleus of the Royal Society (1661) had made England the foremost center of scientific research. Newton's achievements formed the copestone.

Yet this progressive self-reliance and materialism did not necessarily imply the atheism which might have been expected to follow the supplanting of the old, primarily scriptural, authorities by experimental and rationalistic standards. Newton, for instance, turned his principal energies to theology before he was fifty and labored in that field for over thirty years. Indeed, when he was looking back over his life he made an unforgettable comment which illuminates his humility before nature and before nature's God.

I know not what the world will think of my labours, but to myself it seems that I have been but as a child playing on the sea-shore; now finding some pebble rather more polished, and now some shell rather more agreeably variegated than another, while the immense ocean of truth extended itself unexplored before me.

Alexander Pope, that master of epigrammatic statement, was a good deal less humble when he summed up the optimism which stemmed from the discoveries of Locke and Newton in the familiar lines of his *Essay on Man* (1733–38).[11]

> All Nature is but art, unknown to thee;
> All chance, direction, which thou canst not see;
> All discord, harmony not understood;
> All partial evil, universal good:
> And, spite of pride, in erring reason's spite,
> One truth is clear, Whatever is, is right.

Or, as he also said:

> Nature and Nature's laws lay hid in Night;
> God said, Let Newton be, and all was light.

[11] It is a commentary on the new tolerance of his time that Pope was a Catholic.

CHAPTER VI

World Wars for Empire
1689-1783

BRITAIN WAS at war for forty-five of the ninety-four years
between 1689 and 1783. That is not to say that the Island
Kingdom embarked on a systematic career of conquest or
went out of its way to provoke wars. This was in general a
period when there was more war than peace among the
European nations, not only at home, but also in their trade
and colonizing projects in the Americas and India.

Not many Europeans had any very exact idea of how the
outer continents and oceans came to be involved. They
thought in terms of dynastic rivalries, the balance of power,
and of how close France came to complete mastery of their
world, that is, of Europe. They were more interested in
what Britons did to preserve a balance of power on the
Continent than in British acquisition of the most useful
parts of North America and India, Britain's subsequent loss
of thirteen of her American colonies, and the inconspicuous
but systematic and astute way in which the world's greatest
naval power picked up strategic bases like Gibraltar, the
Cape of Good Hope, and the Falkland Islands.[1]

Britons themselves were not much more aware of the
imperial course of their country than were other Europeans.

[1] Covering the sea route between Atlantic and Pacific round Cape Horn.

In fact most British stay-at-homes have usually been so ignorant of, and indifferent to, their empire that they have
been accused of acquiring it absent-mindedly. The truth
appears to be, however, that acquisitive British adventurers
overseas met such feeble opposition that they could hardly
help expanding their various enterprises except when they
came up against European competitors. When that happened they could appeal for home support in European
terms and sometimes get it for that reason. The growth of
the British Empire has been a good deal like a grass fire—
dead or smoldering at the center and blazing only at the
edges.

Britons thought of themselves as a peace-loving people
who were forever being provoked into war by the intolerable pretensions of the French, and then having to defend
their rightful possessions against various French coalitions
with the help of whatever allies they could attract to their
cause. Actually they did manage to keep out of some of the
almost constant European wars, but whenever there seemed
a likelihood of the Continent falling under French domination, they felt impelled to step in. British expenditures for
naval and military enterprise and for subsidies to allies were
colossal by any standard and the national debt grew rapidly,
but somehow the national wealth and strength grew too.[2]

The first period of war was a continuation of the duel between Louis XIV and William of Orange which began in
1672. France, reorganized politically and economically by
Colbert and other able servants of the Sun King, had decided to erase Holland from the European scene and to
appropriate her wealth, commerce, and colonies. William

---

2 England seems to have learned in the sixteenth and seventeenth centuries that war subsidies to allies were more practical than war loans. A national debt of £1,000,000 in 1689 had become over £240,000,000 by 1784.

and the Dutch had warded off this fate by heroic sacrifice, but the odds were still against William when he became King of England. Indeed, if James II had promptly asked Louis to divert William by attacking Holland in 1688, it would have been comparatively easy to prevent the Glorious Revolution. As it was, Colbert's newly created navy thoroughly defeated an Anglo-Dutch fleet off the south coast of England the day before William won the Battle of the Boyne over James's army in Ireland.

The French were so lax in following up this naval success, however, that by 1694, when they decided to invade England in James's behalf, the English and the Dutch were ready for them and in a five-day battle near La Hogue and Cherbourg they practically destroyed the French navy. It did not amount to much for the next fifty years. In North America this war was marked by cruel raids on the Acadian settlements around the Bay of Fundy, a futile attempt to bluff Quebec into surrender, and savage French and Indian attacks on the frontier settlements of New England and New York. The French-Canadians won the upper hand in a series of land and sea expeditions for control of the fur trade around Hudson Bay.

The Peace of Augsburg in 1697 meant that France had been halted in her twenty-five-year campaign of expansion. Territorial matters pretty well reverted to their condition before the war, but Louis agreed to drop his support of James II. Within five years, however, he could not resist an opportunity to place his grandson on the throne of Spain, thus uniting, dynastically at least, the two greatest Continental powers. This meant war and he knew it.[3] William

[3] He invaded the Netherlands, and told the dying James II that he would support the claims of his son to the English throne.

lived barely long enough to unite Austria, Holland, and England against France in 1701–02.

Anne Stuart, William's sister-in-law and successor, was a dull, if stubborn and conscientious, woman whose husband, George of Denmark, was still duller. This couple may have been unfortunate in inheriting a war, but they were blessed in also inheriting a military genius, John Churchill, Earl (later Duke) of Marlborough, to run it for them. This extraordinary man was politician, diplomat, and master of warfare, all in one. He kept his allies in line, his armies in good condition, and his foes perplexed and fearful. His supreme achievement was to break down the stilted and lumbering methods into which land warfare and siege operations had recently lapsed.

Marlborough believed in speed and boldness once he had sized up a situation and prepared for it in detail. With the assistance of his loyal associate, dashing Prince Eugene of Austria, he utterly humiliated France and shattered her armies in four famous battles within five years—Blenheim, Ramillies, Oudenarde, and Malplaquet (1704–09). Had England supported him generously, he might have occupied Paris itself. French children still sing his exploits in "Malbrouck s'en va t'en guerre." [4]

Marlborough fought his campaigns principally in the Low Countries and the Rhine and Danube valleys, but the war went on elsewhere as well. English command of the seas was signalized by the captures of Gibraltar and Minorca as bases for maritime power in the Mediterranean. An alliance was made with Portugal, and Spain was invaded in a futile way from rebel Catalonia.

[4] The English sing "We won't go home till morning" to the same old tune.

Oddly enough, in spite of British numerical and naval superiority, the French clearly held the upper hand in North America. Thanks in large part to the remarkable prowess on land and sea of the brothers of the Le Moyne family of Canada, France practically expelled the English from Hudson Bay, curbed their pretensions in Newfoundland, and won from them and the Spaniards a great race for control of the Mississippi and of the Gulf region at its mouth. A mighty British and colonial plan for the conquest of Canada overland from New York and by sea from New England petered out dismally in 1710 and 1711. Little Port Royal in Acadia (Nova Scotia) was overwhelmed, but the Quebec expedition piled up in stupid and tragic shipwreck on the shoals of the St. Lawrence.

The peace which was made at Utrecht in 1713 reversed the fortunes of war geographically, partly because the British rural aristocracy was determined to end the long war, and partly because England had no territorial ambitions on the Continent. Thus on the European side Great Britain merely secured the recognition of Queen Anne and the repudiation of the Old Pretender (son of James II), a promise that the thrones of France and Spain would never be united, and sovereignty over Gibraltar and Minorca. In the Americas it was quite a different story. Britons took over for thirty years the extremely valuable French monopoly (*Asiento*) of supplying slaves to Spanish America, received the right to send annually a 500-ton ship with trade goods to the Spanish colonies, and obtained Hudson Bay, Newfoundland, and Acadia—three vital outposts of French North America.

This first great bout of war (1689–1713) was followed by twenty-five years of peace, during which what had been a rather tentative pattern of domestic affairs took crisp shape.

The Glorious Revolution, while exhilarating, had created
a precarious situation between the Whig party, whose
achievement it was largely, and the Tories, who had co-
operated chiefly because of their fear of Catholicism. The
two groups probably had more in common than in contra-
diction, but as contending parties they took on certain col-
ors which distinguished them. Thus the Tories were more
unhappy than the Whigs about the Crown passing to a dis-
tant Hanoverian line of the Stuarts after the death of Anne
in 1714,[5] and some of them played more or less seriously
with the idea of restoring the Old Pretender (in 1715) or
"Bonny Prince Charlie," the Young Pretender (in 1745).
The Whigs were more inclined than the stubbornly Anglican Tories to connive at devices whereby Nonconformists
could get round their restricted rights of citizenship. The
Tories were obsessed by domestic and rural affairs, and
characteristically suspicious of Whig preoccupation with
wars, foreign commerce, colonies, and the mysterious ways
of making money from investment in business enterprise
instead of from landed property.

The two parties were almost one, however, in defending,
in behalf of a propertied minority, the Parliamentary sovereignty which they had won in 1689. They put the standing army on a one-year term, renewable only by Parliament
(1689), and reinforced this by limiting the life of any Parliament to three years and by requiring the meeting of Parliament at least once in three years (1694). They prevented
royal domination of the judges by making them removable
only by Parliament (1701). They instituted very high qualifications in landed property for membership in Parliament
(1711), and then gave Members a better chance to profit
from their nearness to the spoils by extending the term of

[5] None of her thirteen children lived to maturity.

Parliament to seven years (1716). They maintained an indefensibly unrepresentative system of electoral constituencies, because these had become a kind of property, and seats
in the Commons could be bought and sold.

Their greatest political achievement was the slow, trial-
and-error invention of the most satisfactory relationship between a representative legislature and its executive which
has yet been discovered. In some senses this invention was
not complete and sure until about 1850, but its underlying
principles emerged early in the eighteenth century. The
King had the unquestioned right to choose his ministers
and counselors, but William and Anne discovered that
there was little use in picking men who could not persuade
Parliament to support their policies. That, in turn, meant
finding men who could command a majority, particularly
in the House of Commons, where ever since the reign of
Charles II two political parties had been competing to form
majorities for their own ends. The natural outcome, therefore, was that if a majority could be organized, the sovereign
was pretty well forced to accept a committee of its leaders
as his Ministry or Government.[6]

Appearance and reality were strangely mixed. All executive action was in the King's name, and by a useful maxim
the King could do no wrong, but Parliament could call a
halt at any time by refusing to vote for the measures of the
King's Ministers who actually exercised his executive
power. This was a more efficient and less ruthless device
for controlling policy than the ancient methods of impeach-
ing individual Ministers or condemning them by bill of at-
tainder. The honorific Privy Council continued to exist
with its dozens of members, but none of them amounted to

[6] William and Anne tried coalition ministries and found them inefficient.

much politically unless he headed a government depart-
ment, and even then he might not belong to the inner working executive, or Cabinet.[7]

Convenience demanded that the Cabinet have a leader,
a First, or Prime, Minister to whom the King might look for
the management of Parliament and to whom Parliament
could turn for explanation and defense of the nation's policies. Since there was a good deal of traditional dislike of
rigid party alignment and of what was called "a formed opposition," and downright suspicion of Cabinet government,
the Prime Minister had a difficult time keeping his majority
in line. The classical solution, then much more than now,
was judicious distribution of the patronage which the King
put at the disposal of his Parliamentary manager.

The first man to be generally recognized (and reviled) as
Prime Minister was Sir Robert Walpole, the Whig leader
and landowner who came to the fore soon after the accession
of the German-born and bred Hanoverian king, George I,
in 1714. George I and his successor of 1727, George II,[8] had
neither the inclination nor the capacity to govern England,
indeed it seems doubtful whether they really understood
how it was governed. Walpole did the job for them by ma-
nipulating men and elections. He did much to establish
the convention that Cabinet members must form a solid
front to Parliament or resign from the group. He made use
of the postwar moods of conservatism, moderation, pacifism,
and caution. He concurred in the prevailing reverence for
property and all kinds of vested interest, and for their chief
bulwark, the common law. He encouraged the prevailing

[7] So named because they were few enough to meet in a small room.
[8] George II gave Walpole No. 10 Downing Street and Walpole passed it
on to his successors.

pride in the liberty of the individual in relation to the state and in the freedom of speech and expression which went with it.

In brief, Walpole cultivated the complacency which descended upon the ruling British oligarchy after a generation during which they had not only made their Glorious Revolution work profitably, but had also checked France. He kept the Tories fairly quiet while the Whigs managed national policies by letting them have a monopoly of local administration. His motto "Let sleeping dogs lie" was thoroughly appropriate to his times.

For one thing, the country was making money hand over fist, as the scale of her own naval and military expenditures and her large subsidies to her allies had testified. London was a humming hive of commerce and finance. It and part of the nation had been briefly infected by the mania for speculation which was born in Europe early in the eighteenth century, the offspring of paper money and joint-stock companies. Indeed Walpole had earned his first pre-eminence by his skill and honesty in rescuing the country from the distress which followed the pricking of "the South Sea bubble" of 1720.[9] Thereafter the capital had settled down to more sober ways of exploiting an expanding domestic economy and foreign trade. The East India Company had by now left the Dutch far behind and was building scores of great English fortunes. Fisheries, colonies, carrying trade, and slave trade created more.

The whole productive apparatus was clothed in an elaborate set of mercantilistic regulations which were designed to balance colonial production of noncompetitive products (chiefly raw materials) against British manufacturing, proc-

[9] The South Sea Company was an inflated structure based upon the *Asiento* monopoly.

essing, and middleman commerce, and meanwhile to restrict the carrying trade to British and colonial shipping.
Yet there was an elastic practicality about the whole structure which made it more effective than the more rigid apparatus of Spain, France, and Holland. In addition, by
concentrating on the production of good cheap staples like
woolens, hardware, tobacco, and rum, Britons not only captured more and more overseas markets for themselves but
also provided unscrupulous Spanish and French colonists
with cheaper and more attractive goods than their home
countries could deliver. Scotland, having failed disastrously
to found an empire of her own at the end of the seventeenth
century, had found it very profitable to get inside the English system by means of the union of the two kingdoms to
form Great Britain which was effected in 1707.

Wealth bred leisure, and the leisured encouraged the arts
of civilization. Voltaire visited England from 1726 to 1729
and felt compelled to tell Europe what a marvelous place
it was. "When one considers," he wrote, "that Newton
would have been persecuted in France, imprisoned at
Rome, and burned at Lisbon, what are we to think of human reason? One would swear that reason was a native of
England in the present age at least." Naturally, complacent
Britons tried to live up to this and other flattering foreigners' impressions. At Bath, Beau Nash drilled high society
in the niceties of a dignified and stoical social behavior.
Architecture aimed at classical simplicity and symmetry.
Dr. Johnson tutored the upper classes in exact expression;
the essayists (save the misanthropic Jonathan Swift) enter-
tained and instructed them in a cool, balanced prose; and
Garrick fed them Shakespeare. Brilliant Scotsmen like
Hume, Robertson, and Adam Smith conquered a great sec-
tor of British intellectual life for themselves and later fel-

low countrymen. Gibbon crowned the period and awed Europe by the scholarship and polished artistry of his *Decline and Fall of the Roman Empire* (published 1776–88), which was also a consummate reflection of the skeptical rationalism of his own times. Young men made the Grand Tour of Europe and planted there the stereotype of the "milord anglais," much as American "millionaires" impressed themselves on Europe two centuries later, for they bought up all sorts of objects of art and carried home foreign fashions in clothes and behavior.

Needless to say, the ideal of reason, moderation, and stoic dignity was often offended. The country squires were a boorish lot of petty local tyrants who were obsessed with hunting, wenching, and drinking. In spite of Beau Nash, the tempers and passions of the governing oligarchy could be violent. And the masses of the nation, particularly in London and the large towns, while certainly the most fortunate people in Europe, were being badly debauched by the substitution of cheap, potent gin for the malt brews formerly popular. It is the presence of this violence below a veneer of restraint which leads the English historian G. M. Trevelyan to observe that "with a very small army and no effective police, the British State might at this period have been defined as aristocracy tempered by rioting." Indeed the Riot Act, so famous in English-speaking countries, dates from 1715.[10] The marvelous pictorial dramas of English life which the painter and engraver William Hogarth produced between 1720 and 1760 portray an England turbulent from top to bottom with energies which were frequently of a very sordid kind.

---

[10] G. M. Trevelyan, *History of England* (New York, 1928), p. 533. To "read the Riot Act" means a command by a public official for twelve or more persons to disperse.

Walpole did his best to avoid the second round of wars which began in 1739 and lasted with some interruptions until 1783, but British adventurers overseas had become embroiled with Spaniards and Frenchmen and had suffered reprisals which were used at home to influence public opinion. With the connivance of Spanish-American colonists, the quotas of the *Asiento* had been flagrantly exceeded, and, when Spanish officials and coast guards tried to tighten up the controls, some violent clashes took place. Trouble was also brewing on the frontiers between British Georgia and Spanish Florida, between the coastal American colonies and the French in the Mississippi valley and Great Lakes basin, and also "down East" in the vicinity of Nova Scotia and Newfoundland, where the French had retrieved some of their losses under the treaty of Utrecht by building the mightiest fortress in North America at Louisbourg on Cape Breton Island and excluding New Englanders from a magnificent fishery. Out in India and around the Indian Ocean the British and French East India Companies were sparring for advantage.

In 1739 a certain Captain Jenkins, who carried around with him a well-dried ear which he said had been torn off his head by Spanish coast guards, thereby provided the excuse for a declaration of war against Spain. Within a year, this war was merged in a dynastic European conflict arising from the attempt of Prussia to diminish Austrian predominance over the German states. That war lasted until 1748, lapsed into a futile, uneasy peace for seven or eight years, and then flamed out again until 1763. Again there was a period of peace until the American Revolution began and drew in France, Spain, and Holland, until another peace was concluded in 1783.

In these wars Great Britain hastened the decline of Spain

and the Spanish Empire and stripped France of most of her empire overseas, only to have her European rivals turn upon her for the glorious revenge of assisting thirteen British colonies in North America to achieve their independence. In 1763 Britons looked out on a world where their only imperial rival was Spain. Twenty years later they had managed to lose the whole of eastern North America between Nova Scotia and Florida to a shaky, but independent, federation called the United States of America—the first of their offspring to sever the family ties.

Britain took part in the European wars of this period by means of her navy, several armies, and large subsidies to her allies. At home she had to deal in 1745 with a romantic lost cause in the form of a Scottish rising and invasion of England led by James II's grandson, Charles Stuart. Thanks largely to her naval and financial strength, the European side of the wars went on the whole favorably. Gibraltar and Minorca were all that Britons wanted in Europe beyond the British Isles. The French and Spanish navies were repeatedly humbled and Britain's new and almost too formidable ally, Frederick the Great of Prussia, miraculously emerged from various alliances against him to stand as an imposing counterpoise to France on the Continent. Russia, another new leading actor, could be balanced against Austria and Prussia.

The great changes in the British position took place overseas in North America and in India—a circumstance which was neatly symbolized in the interim peace treaty of 1748 when Louisbourg, which had been captured by New Englanders and the British navy, was restored to France in exchange for Madras on the eastern coast of India, which had been captured by the French Governor of Pondicherry

and the French navy. It is also worth recalling that Elihu
Yale contributed to the founding of the Connecticut college
which bears his name with wealth secured as Governor of
Madras, and was succeeded in that office by a Harvard man.
Columbia University rounded out an academic reflection
of changing relationships in the British Empire. Founded
as King's College in New York by George II, it adopted its
more republican name after the Revolution, while some of
its vanquished royalist elements were setting up a new
King's College in Nova Scotia, the still loyal North American province in which they found refuge.

The years between 1744 and 1763 saw a gradual triumph
of the English cause over France and Spain in the West
Indies and eastern North America. At first the French distinctly held their own and administered some humiliating
defeats, except in Nova Scotia where Halifax was founded
in 1749 as a counterpoise to Louisbourg. The truth was
that stubborn intercolonial jealousies defeated the efforts
of colonial statesmen to create an American union which
might easily have defeated the French in North America,
and this at a time when Great Britain was hamstrung by the
corrupt inefficiency into which Parliamentary government
had descended.

The House of Commons contained in William Pitt [11] the
fiery patriot and honest organizing genius who could defeat
France, but the nation could not use his abilities until he
had struck a reluctant bargain with the Parliamentary
"boss," the Duke of Newcastle. As soon as Pitt and Pitt's
men got to work, the tide turned. Louisbourg and Fort
Duquesne (Pittsburgh) fell in 1758, and Quebec was captured by James Wolfe's daring in 1759. In that year also

[11] Grandson of a governor of Madras.

the navy smashed the French Atlantic and Mediterranean fleets,[12] so that it was the British navy which sailed up the St. Lawrence in 1760, thus sealing the fate of Montreal and New France. These and further triumphs in the West Indies [13] explain why by the treaty of 1763 France lost her North American empire except for two small islands near Newfoundland and a remnant of her West Indian possessions, and why Great Britain superseded Spain in Florida. France compensated Spain with Louisiana, but the eastern and northern halves of North America were now both British.

Events in India followed the same triumphant course, somewhat to the embarrassment of the East India Company. It, like the Hudson's Bay Company, was resolutely opposed to becoming a territorial power. It had developed an exceedingly profitable peaceful commerce and all it wanted was quiet possession of useful trading posts or "factories" at various points on the coast. On the other hand, the French East India Company, which was not doing so well and which shrewdly estimated French naval inferiority, hit upon the idea of involving itself in the politics of the distressed and divided Indian states so as to use Indian land forces to expel the Britons.

François Dupleix, the French governor, had been pursuing this policy with considerable success for about ten years when the rebound came. Robert Clive, a young clerk of the English company, revealed himself to be a daring, brilliant soldier who in less than three years (1751–53) beat Dupleix at his own game. When Anglo-French war broke out again in 1756, Clive's successes in Bengal were even more spectacular, as his small, well-trained forces defeated

12 And also destroyed at Le Havre an invasion fleet of flatboats.
13 The captures of Havana from Spain and of a number of French islands.

Indian armies twenty or twenty-five times their size. In this war naval co-operation enabled British land forces elsewhere in India to erase French power completely. These twenty years of embroilment in Indian politics, and the enormous loot and indemnities which accompanied its successes, ended once and for all the company's policy of refusing to expand beyond the factories. Thereafter Britons were committed to direct or indirect territorial power over an ever-increasing number of Indian states, while the French were confined to the relative inferiority of their restored trading posts.

Britain's triumph in the peace treaties of 1763, which made her the greatest empire in the world, was a colossal one, the like of which had never been seen before, but it was to be dimmed within twenty years by the unexpected rise to independence of thirteen of the North American colonies, which were now freed from the menace of France in North America. The complicated strife and interplay both within Great Britain and North America, and between them, from which the United States emerged, presents a fascinating drama. Hundreds of books and articles have been devoted to examining its many aspects, and even today there are many different interpretations of the facts.

A simple and revealing formula for understanding the American Revolution is to compare the situation to a family one. The thirteen colonies were like children who had grown up. Great Britain was like a parent who stubbornly and stupidly refused to admit it. The only thing for the dominant groups in the colonies to do was to try to set up a separate establishment. France, Spain, and Holland were like neighbors who cherished an ancient grudge against John Bull and, by taking his children's side, ensured their success.

Actually the brilliant leading American statesmen were like lean and athletic disciples of John Locke contending with a paunchy priesthood which had perverted the fighting creed of the Glorious Revolution into an empty, decadent ritual. Benjamin Franklin, for instance, had spent over twenty years trying to make Britons understand that they must grant the reality instead of the appearance of self-government to colonies which were so mature politically and economically, and he hoped up to the very last that this plain truth might penetrate closed British minds. The American leaders were simply and quite reasonably asking for what Canadians demanded and got seventy years later and what they subsequently developed into the voluntary association of constitutional equals in the British Commonwealth of today.[14] It was to take two generations, marked by the loss of the American colonies, a political revolution at home, the abandonment of mercantilism in favor of free trade, and two Canadian rebellions, before the governing class in Great Britain saw the light. It is notable, however, that they were the first imperial people since the ancient Greeks to see it.

While the underlying cause of the American Revolution was the inability of Great Britain to organize her empire after 1763 in such a way as to concede whole-heartedly the local autonomy which the more substantial American colonies were determined and ready to have, most of the Americans who made the Revolution were urged on by the sense of more particular grievances. It was not to be expected that many of them would think of the problem in British terms, that is, as postwar centralization and recon-

---

[14] Madison, looking back from 1800, said: "The fundamental principle of the revolution was that the Colonies were coordinate members with each other and with Great Britain, of an Empire united by a common executive sovereign."

struction of empire old and new in order to recoup some of the enormous wartime expenditures which were burdening the taxpayer. The colonists were suffering from postwar depression themselves, and this aggravated certain regional complaints.

New England and the Middle Colonies had hitherto ignored and evaded lax British mercantilistic controls, thereby building up, and becoming dependent upon, intricate, interlocked structures of domestic production and of foreign trade with the West Indies, Africa, and Europe. If Britain should tighten up her imperial regulation of commerce and the carrying trade, she would find that some of her colonies had become self-confident competitors. The Southern planters, who exchanged their staple products for British manufactures, had fallen deeply into debt, partly because of their luxurious tastes, but basically because they had been effectively exploited by British businessmen. The Southerners, therefore, wanted easy money and debt easements just when London was bent upon rigidly orthodox finance. The Western frontiersmen, whose democratic tendencies made them at least as hostile to British oligarchy as to their own tidewater overlords, wanted the opportunity and the speculative profits which they believed had been opened to them by the conquest of the French lands between the Appalachian ranges and the Mississippi; but British policy, more sensitive to the need for reducing friction between whites and Indians, was committed to reducing the entry of American pioneers to a minimum.

These contradictions developed into burning issues in rapid succession after 1763, and the British Parliament met them by declaring that the colonial legislatures were "subordinate" and "dependent" and that it had "full power and authority to make laws and statutes of sufficient force and

validity to bind the colonies and people of America . . .
in all cases whatsoever." American hostility to British policy
quickly progressed from riotous defeats of new taxes and
more rigid controls to skillfully organized boycotts and
other forms of resistance. Clashes with officials were followed by destruction and bloodshed when military and
naval forces became involved. Gradually the American determination hardened to deny Parliamentary authority and
to meet the consequences if Parliament tried to impose its
will by force. George III and his ministers had no thought
of giving in. Thirteen of the colonies proclaimed their independence on July 4, 1776.

When war came, the British commanders began timidly
and tentatively, in the expectation that the issues could be
resolved peacefully if there was no great bloodshed. Although American resistance was weak and sporadic at first,
it was somehow persistently maintained by the loose con-
federation of the colonies and by the remarkable steadfast-
ness of General George Washington. American invasions
of Canada and Nova Scotia failed for want of naval support,
but a British counterinvasion from Montreal ended in disastrous surrender at Saratoga on the upper Hudson in 1777,
because of the breakdown of the long lines of communica-
tion. That American victory won French alliance and financial support, soon to be followed by similar aid from
Spain and Holland.

British armies, operating under naval control of the Atlantic coast, were able to campaign and to win battles almost wherever they pleased, but they could not find a way
of extinguishing American resistance in the North, in the
Middle Colonies, or the South. The huge area was too
large to be dominated from the other side of the Atlantic,
and Washington wisely refused to oblige his opponents by

lining up all his forces for a fight to a finish. Suddenly, in the early autumn of 1781, after six years of exhausting, indecisive campaigning, the French alliance weighed down the scales on the American side. The British navy was in decline; the French navy in the ascendant, with Spain and Holland helping. While a French squadron under De Grasse controlled the mouth of Chesapeake Bay, Washington and his French military allies quickly gathered in Virginia to outnumber the main British army two to one at Yorktown. The British commander, Lord Cornwallis, surrendered on October 19th, and the American war was over. Next year Admiral Rodney obtained his revenge over De Grasse by a great victory in the West Indies, and France and Spain gave up their three-year siege of Gibraltar. Yet the American cause had triumphed in time, and American independence was recognized by Great Britain in September, 1782, in a singularly generous preliminary treaty of peace and territorial concession.

The British Parliament between 1760 and 1780 was a lamentable sovereign for the British Empire.[15] It is tempting to lay most of the blame for this on George III, an obstinate and industrious, but short-sighted king, because of the disturbing effects of his attempts to find a Parliamentary manager who would pay more attention to his wishes than Walpole and Newcastle had paid to those of George I and George II. He "gloried," he said, "in the name of Briton," and he saw no reason why he should not use his control of the patronage to create a majority party of "the King's Friends." Then he might at least share real sovereignty in Great Britain as well as reign there. As the constitution stood at that time, this was a quite legitimate, if unfortunate, aspiration, and George III did ultimately obtain a fatal

15 Burke told them so: "A great empire and little minds go ill together."

amount of influence on policy; but he need never have affected it decisively had the Members of Parliament been in general much more enlightened than he was. Most of them never saw beyond the fact that the King wanted to get rid of the Whig control of Parliament.

For twenty years after 1760, during which the problems of North America and India ought to have evoked the highest statesmanship, Parliament devoted itself chiefly to a fascinating and complicated series of inner struggles. The King's patronage was a potent force. The unreformed constituency system had become so antiquated and corrupt that it was estimated that a majority of the House of Commons was elected by only six thousand voters, and that 487 out of 658 members were virtually nominated. Pitt, who everyone knew had engineered the recent surge of victory, gradually retired from his unquestioned primacy in Parliament, partly because of his almost insane personal pride and partly because of the King's obvious ambition to dictate national policies. The brilliant demagogue John Wilkes, who tried to use the freedom of the press and his own status as a Member of Parliament to check the King in his new course, was most flagrantly abused and thwarted by his fellow Members.[16] Between 1760 and 1770 the King never succeeded in getting a Ministry completely to his own taste, but the very fact that there were seven of them showed how Parliament was breaking down into factions.

Success crowned the King's efforts in January, 1770, when Lord North formed a Ministry for him, but it proved to be a success which carried in itself the seeds of failure, that is, the loss of the American colonies and thereby the effective discrediting of George III's design. North did the King's

[16] Americans named the town of Wilkes-Barre after him and another of their British defenders.

work, even though from 1776 onwards he believed that war against the colonies "must end in ruin to his Majesty and the country." During these years Parliament had only itself to blame for putting party politics above the noble appeals to statesmanship in behalf of the Americans which were made by Pitt, Fox, and Burke. Parliament finally realized this, too late, in 1780, when the Commons carried John Dunning's resolution "that it is necessary to declare that the influence of the crown has increased, is increasing, and ought to be diminished." This blunt check to the King and the reassertion of Cabinet authority and ministerial responsibility which followed it were probably the only outstandingly beneficial effects of the American Revolution on Great Britain, but it may well be that they were almost worth the price in their stimulus to Parliamentary reform.

CHAPTER VII

War Arrests Reform
1783–1815

THE BRITISH people may have seemed during the eighteenth century to have locked themselves into a set of congealed and complacent conventions of life, but their underlying vigor made it inevitable that there should be many new warm currents welling up to break through the ice. A number of these were the still-living springs of radicalism which had burst forth during the contest with the Stuarts, only to be capped by the conservative masters of the Revolutionary settlement after 1688. Naturally such springs still found some outlet in Nonconformist circles, for the underprivileged have a way of cherishing what their masters would like to suppress.

Other currents of change were less directly related to the stirring contests of the seventeenth century. Indeed one whole group of them formed a kind of backwash from France. While Britons had been rather lazily preening themselves over the outspoken French admiration for things British, French thinkers had continued to forge ahead. The outcome was that about the time when few of the British upper classes could see beyond the confused turmoil of Parliament during George III's experiments, Frenchmen were publicizing persuasive fresh and revolutionary elements in European thought—political, economic, and philosophical. Britons were suddenly to be awakened to the necessity of accommodating these elements or suppressing them.

Among the currents of change in the field of politics, there was the seventeenth-century Leveler demand for outright manhood suffrage, irrespective of property qualifications. This had been kept alive by Nonconformists and it emerged crisply in 1776, that extraordinary year, in the form of Major John Cartwright's pamphlet *Take Your Choice*.[1] Cartwright spent the rest of his life fighting alone or through political associations for this cause, but at the time of his death in 1824 he had made no appreciable impression on the governing class.

Their utmost concessions to the self-reform of a decadent Parliamentary system had been discussions of the demands put forth after Dunning's resolution of 1780 for some reform of the constituency system and for destruction of the King's grasp on Parliament through patronage. The campaign for constituency reform had been initiated by the elder Pitt in 1770 and taken up by his brilliant second son, William, who became Tory Prime Minister in 1783 at the age of twenty-four. Even he could not persuade Parliament to reform itself, however, and the cause became merely a plank in the platform of the Whig Opposition during the 'nineties. Thanks to the bitterness against George III because of the outcome of the American Revolution, Burke's Economical Reform Act of 1782 did strip the Crown of a large part of its power to corrupt and influence Parliament.

The American Revolution had one other important political repercussion in the British Isles, when Ireland,

[1] Two years earlier, this professional soldier had published *American Independence the Glory and Interest of Great Britain.*

England's oldest dominion, seized upon the occasion to burst at least some of her bonds. Ever since the Battle of the Boyne, Parliament had both facilitated exploitation of Ireland and blocked Irish efforts at economic advancement.[2] Protestants in Ireland, with Catholic support, took advantage of British vulnerability during the American Revolution to raise an enormous volunteer force, whose existence, coupled with the menace from France, strengthened the demands that Ireland's economy and the Irish Parliament be freed from British controls. The second demand was conceded with some substantial limitations in 1782, and Catholics received the vote (although not the right to be Members of Parliament) in 1793.[3]

These and other promising developments were suddenly checked, however, by the moods and fears which were aroused by the French Revolution. Within Ireland Protestants and Catholics ended their profitable coalition, and the latter rebelled when opportunity seemed to beckon from triumphant Revolutionary France. French aid failed. The sad old religious division evoked savage massacre on both sides. Pitt aimed a statesmanlike solution of the whole problem by bringing Ireland, like Scotland, into the Union, by embarking on widespread economic reforms, and by abolishing Catholic civil and political disabilities. George III gave his assent to the union with Ireland, which was formed in 1800, but he would not agree to "Catholic" Emancipation, as it was called, on the ground that his coronation oath bound him to uphold the Anglican establishment, and Pitt resigned. Full citizenship was denied to

2 Even Swift's savage pamphleteering in their behalf had had little lasting effect.

3 They already possessed it in Grenada and the British North American colonies and might be Members of those colonial Parliaments.

Irish and British Roman Catholics for another twenty-eight years.[4]

Yet another wellspring of change in Great Britain was a liking for sentiment—pleasure and trust in human feeling and emotion—which had never died out, but which had been frowned upon by the stoical upper classes after 1660. In spite of disapproval from above, this kind of thing lived on because it was native in the British peoples. It could be found in painting, both portraiture and landscape; it burst forth as a lively lampoon on Italian music in John Gay's *Beggar's Opera,* or, with grave dignity, in the sonorous choral emotions of Handel; and it pervaded a large amount of the poetry and fiction of the eighteenth century. Poets of sentiment like Gray and Goldsmith, and Bishop Percy, the collector of ancient popular ballads, prepared the way for the mystical genius of William Blake and the earthy genius of Robert Burns. In fiction sentiment succeeded best when it slopped over into sentimentality, as witness the popularity of Samuel Richardson's many volumes, or the "best-sellers" in mildly alarming horror and mystery of M. G. Lewis and Mrs. Ann Radcliffe.[5]

In many ways the most winning example of persistent human sentiment was the evangelical, or Wesleyan, movement which welled up within a fossilized Church of England and which ran parallel to the more obscure spiritual

[4] This crisis provoked the third temporary attack of the insanity in George III which became permanent in 1811. The five leading British North American colonies, later comprised in Canada, continued to be saddled with the type of colonial government against which the Americans and the Irish had rebelled. In 1773 a Regulating Act established Parliamentary authority over the now territorial East India Company, and another in 1784 left the company in control of its own commerce and lucrative patronage, but entrusted political control to a member of the British Cabinet.

[5] Richardson had a great, if short-lived, influence in France and a more lasting one in Germany.

companionship in the Nonconformist congregations. John and Charles Wesley, while at Oxford in the late 'twenties of the eighteenth century, turned away from empty formalism towards simplicity, fervor, and experiential religion. At first (notably while missionaries in Georgia) intolerant of Nonconformists, the Wesleys quickly became apostles to all who would seek salvation through faith in Jesus Christ alone. They visited prisons and the sick, and preached in the streets or open fields. They won other great preachers like George Whitefield and Francis Asbury (the Wesley of North America) to their cause, and the system of lay preachers forwarded it still more. It reached Ireland in 1747, stirred Scotland after 1750, and became a powerful force in North America from the 'sixties onwards. John Wesley intended his "Methodist societies" to exist within the Church of England, but when he himself ordained ministers, he had truly broken away, whether he denied it or not. Thanks to his long life, he had organized Methodism securely when he died in 1791, and he left behind him as well a powerful evangelical movement within the Anglican church.

Other omens of change could be found in two books which were published in England in 1776 and which owed a good deal to the intellectual advances which had recently been made in France. These were Jeremy Bentham's *Fragment on Government* and Adam Smith's *Inquiry into the Nature and Causes of the Wealth of Nations*. Bentham was a disciple of the French philosopher Helvétius, and believed that society might be brought close to perfection by wise legislation. Since men irresistibly seek their own advantage and avoid pain, he argued, a scientific structure of penal laws would easily direct their activities to public advantage. That scientific structure could be based upon a

single principle—utility, that is, the contribution of any
course of behavior to the greatest happiness (or good) of the
greatest number.

Smith, on the other hand, had been much interested in a
harmony between his own theory that all moral sentiments
arise from sympathy and the theories of the French Physi-
ocrats concerning social wealth. His revolutionary contribution to British thought was to denounce governmental
interference with the free international exchange of commodities, in fact to denounce nearly all governmental economic regulation except such as was calculated to increase
the armed strength and defensive power of nations. Taking
his cue from the division of labor in industry and from his
conception of man's naturally sympathetic social behavior,
he argued that if each man were permitted to pursue his
own economic self-interest free of legal restrictions he
would be "led by an invisible hand" to promote the public
good.

Clearly Bentham and Smith were logically opposed in
their view of the state, one depending on it to legislate for
human happiness, the other aiming to reduce its interference to a minimum, but since both of them furnished
arguments against the existing structure, both were freely
and often carelessly cited by subsequent generations of
critics. As we shall see, however, each had his own special
uses and the principles of state intervention or noninter-
vention were simply applied in different fields. Trouble
arose only when either "rugged individualism" or "state
socialism" was appealed to as a cure-all.

The French Revolution, which began so auspiciously in
May, 1789, and which ran rapidly through phases of constitutional monarchy, republicanism, democracy, and dictatorship, shook conservative Great Britain like an earth-

quake. When the bonds of authority in France were snapped, new and disruptive ideas were set loose in every field of human speculation from religion and politics to chemistry and military affairs.

Most influential of all were the ideas of the queer French-Swiss genius, Jean Jacques Rousseau. Where Locke had declared that men were born equal, Rousseau asserted that they were born good. He boldly substituted sentiment for rational analysis, the natural morality of the heart for the artificial morality of the mind.[6] He, more than any other individual, gave France the noble creed of Liberty, Equality, and Fraternity. Into the world he launched his belief in unlimited democracy far more conspicuously and persuasively than the English Levelers had done, for he clothed the sovereign voice of the majority of the people with a philosophy of natural human rightness. Rousseau for the first time placed the common man in the center of the world's stage.

At the beginning of the Revolution, British opinion was favorable, for it looked as if the French were acknowledging British wisdom by imitation. But when the revolutionaries progressively struck at property rights, democratized the constitution, executed the King and Queen, and guillotined not only the aristocrats but also the moderates, fear united the British governing classes into a compact and almost unanimous group. Burke (with a large following) transferred his allegiance from the Whig party to its natural home among the Tories, and in November, 1790, he published his condemnatory *Reflections on the Revolution in France, and on the proceedings in certain societies in London relative to that event.*

[6] He had reveled in the writings of Richardson.

Among many others,[7] the irrepressible Tom Paine re-
plied, with the shrewd and trenchant *Rights of Man,* but
there was little use in fighting against the tide, for the
upper classes rallied to the conservative creed so eloquently
stated by Burke. Authority began to strike against every
manifestation of sympathy with the novelties and excesses
across the Channel. The younger Pitt, who was on the
threshold of the political power which would have enabled
him to push through far-reaching reforms,[8] was utterly defeated in these aims by the temper of his class, who viewed
any hint of change as Jacobinism, that is, as subversive and
unpatriotic. A succession of laws eliminated long-cherished
liberties of the citizen to assemble, discuss, study, form
trade unions, and express opinion. Habeas corpus was
suspended, and spies and provocative agents honeycombed
every kind of popular organization. About the only evidences of the old free spirit and the new ideas of reform
were two achievements of the leader of the Whigs, Charles
James Fox—the Libel Act of 1792 [9] and Abolition of the
Slave Trade in 1807—and the courage of an occasional jury.

Napoleon Bonaparte, said Anatole France, was the French
Revolution in military boots. Certainly Britons thought so,
for this military genius, who set no limits on his designs for
world power, made it clear from the beginning that he
would harness all the energies recently released in France
and all the support which he could squeeze out of conquered
nations in order to subdue Great Britain and the British
Empire. In this he was shrewder than Louis XIV. No one

[7] Notably the founder of modern feminism, Mary Wollstonecraft, and her
later husband, William Godwin, the founder of philosophical anarchism.

[8] He advocated a system of compulsory national social insurance, education, and so on.

[9] Which gave juries full competence in libel cases.

could dominate Europe then, still less the world, as long as Britons had the strength to bar the way by military and naval enterprise, by aid to Continental resistance, and by the productive capacities which were geared to their world commerce. By his unremitting menace for almost twenty years, Napoleon crystallized for a long time to come that British reliance on naval power and economic mobilization which had emerged in Elizabethan times and had taken clear form in the days of William III and Marlborough.

The wars of the French Revolution began in the spring of 1792 and ended on the field of Waterloo in June, 1815. Britain was almost continuously involved from February, 1793, onwards, her primary concern being over control of the Low Countries and her earliest role that of "paymaster" to the encircling coalition which Revolutionary France had challenged. For four years matters went thoroughly badly for Britain. The Coalition was ridden with dissension, the French easily overwhelmed hopelessly led British armies in the Low Countries, young Bonaparte devised a way to drive them out of Toulon, and West Indian yellow fever destroyed British soldiers and sailors alike. By the middle of 1797, the only British successes had been an ineffective naval victory off Brest and assumption of control over the former Dutch possessions at Cape of Good Hope and Ceylon. Napoleon had just knocked out Austria, leaving Britain the sole survivor of the Coalition, and mutiny was running like wildfire through the British navy.

Yet during the last half of 1797 that same navy turned the tide in the Battle of Britain, just as the Royal Air Force was to do a century and a half later. Spencer and Jervis and Nelson shattered the fleets of France's allies—the Spaniards off Cape St. Vincent and the Dutch at Camperdown. Efforts to strike at Britain from Ireland failed. In 1798, when Bonaparte made his first attempt to destroy Britain's accretion of power from India by invading the land bridge to India in Egypt, Nelson destroyed his whole fleet by an astounding bit of originality in battle at the mouth of the Nile. Three years later, when Bonaparte inveigled Russia into an alliance to break Britain by denying her access to the trade and naval stores of northern Europe, Nelson did the trick again by threading a shallow channel to destroy the satellite Danish fleet at Copenhagen.[10] In 1802, the uneasy Peace of Amiens furnished a breathing spell for the master of the Continent and the foe who still eluded his reach.

Hostilities were resumed in 1803, technically because Britain had broken the recent treaty by not surrendering the valuable naval base at Malta, but at least as much because Napoleon was ready to invade England. Incredible as it may seem in an age of sail, the British navy blockaded the French fleets at Toulon and Brest for twenty months, thus preventing them from uniting to cover the invasion fleet which was waiting at Boulogne. This service played the devil with wooden ships, but it bred sailors. When the French ships finally escaped and joined the Spaniards at Cadiz, they formed a fleet of thirty-three ships of the line to Nelson's twenty-seven, yet the brilliant Englishman utterly routed them off Trafalgar, near Gibraltar, on October 21, 1805. Nelson was killed in this battle. His great master, Pitt, then Prime Minister for the second time, was not long to survive him. He had just formed another coalition with Austria and Russia, but Napoleon destroyed the

10 It was here that Nelson managed to ignore a recall signal by putting his telescope to his blind eye. At the Nile he had "sandwiched" and destroyed the long line of French ships anchored close to shore by sending one column of his own ships inside, and one outside of them.

Austrian and Russian armies before the year was over, and the exhausted Pitt gave out.[11]

The last phase of the wars was at bottom stubborn blockade and counterblockade, a course which brought the United States most unprofitably in on Napoleon's side in 1812. Great Britain tried to prevent Continental trade with the outside world except through British controls. Napoleon dragooned all Europe into his "Continental System" in order to dry up the flow of Britain's economic lifeblood.

With Britain seizing American vessels which tried to trade with the French-controlled Continent or West Indies, and Napoleon seizing those which submitted to British search or touched at a British port, the United States was hard hit. President Jefferson met the situation by the already characteristic American policy of neutrality, supplemented in this case by an embargo on all foreign commerce, but his policies had failed by the time Madison succeeded him in 1809. Widespread economic distress and intense bitterness over arrogant British searches of American vessels, either for contraband or in order to impress alleged British deserters, were supplemented by the cocksure expansionism of American Westerners who thought they saw an excellent chance to annex Canada and Florida. Madison declared war in 1812 without knowing that Great Britain had decided a few days earlier to lighten her naval controls and to mollify the United States.

Napoleon's Continental System broke down first. The Baltic was kept open by destroying a second Danish fleet. British blockade runners were everywhere. British armies struck at French armies of occupation through Portugal

---

[11] He died on January 23, 1806, the twenty-fifth anniversary of his entry to the Commons. His opponent Fox died September 13, 1806, just after carrying his motion for abolition of the slave trade.

and Spain in the bitter six-year Peninsular War which converted the Indian veteran Sir Arthur Wellesley, later Duke
of Wellington, into a master of strategy and tactics. Northern Europe grew restless under the Continental System,
and finally Czar Alexander determined to withdraw from it.

In 1812 Napoleon, like his emulator Hitler in 1941, decided that he must prove to the Russians who was master of
Europe. His attempt was an unmitigated disaster because
he could not destroy the Russian armies, whereas the Russians and their country's climate could destroy his. In 1813,
Wellington finally broke through the Pyrenees into France,
and in mid-Europe the combined armies of Russia, Prussia,
and Austria defeated the weakened Napoleon at Leipzig,
forcing him to abdicate and retire to Elba in 1814. Next
year he escaped, resumed his French imperial throne, and
faced a circle of enemies. He chose to meet them at Waterloo near Brussels, where Wellington's army, in its disciplined formations of line and square, fought all day, breaking massed assaults and counterattacking, until Marshal
Blücher tipped the balance decisively by arriving with his
Prussians, and Napoleon fled.[12]

The French emperor was exiled to lonely St. Helena,
and the diplomats who had started to reconstruct Europe
the year before at Vienna resumed their work. Thanks to
the British record and to Wellington's prestige, Lord Castle-
reagh was able to get essentially what his country wanted,
that is, the tranquilization of Europe and the reconstruction of a balance among the powers which would leave Great
Britain free to recuperate from her exhausting efforts. Thus
France was re-established with practically no loss of territory,

---

[12] Appropriately, Thomas Hardy's *The Dynasts* (1904–06), one of the
greatest English literary works since Milton, commemorates in original and
penetrating form the ordeals of the Napoleonic era.

and London lent her the money to pay an indemnity for Napoleon's last outburst. Continental diplomats, eagerly bargaining over legitimism and European territorial adjustments, were not a little puzzled by the obsession of the British agents, egged on by powerful evangelical forces at home, with securing the abolition of the slave trade.

This seemed to them to be an inexpensive concession, as did concurrence in Britain's strange passion for out-of-the-way fragments of the earth's surface. Britons could have almost anything of this sort they wanted. They chose to take the Cape of Good Hope, Mauritius, Ceylon, Heligoland, Malta (in place of Minorca), the Ionian Islands, a piece of Guiana, Trinidad, and a few West Indian islands. Australia had been developed as a penal settlement in 1788, because the American colonies were no longer available for this purpose, and British commercial enterprise had begun in New Zealand, Singapore, Hong Kong, and British Columbia. That is, in 1815, British stay-at-homes were satisfied by the re-establishment of a balance among the powers on the Continent, while the makers of naval and commercial policy used the occasion to pick up a selection of valuable bases for future operations. In North America, the War of 1812, which had almost split the United States and had brought her into serious straits, was terminated by restoration of the *status quo ante* and the reference of certain territorial problems to joint commissions.

Looking back on the achievements of the years between 1783 and 1815, it is obvious that there must have been both enormous economic strength in Great Britain and skillful organization of it. Napoleon called the English "a nation of shopkeepers." The sneer can be ignored, for British commerce, which was the taproot of British strength and growth, was not without courageous enterprise, and the vigor which flowed from that root was the principal agent of Napoleon's failure. And, when the French emperor tried to make France and the rest of Europe get along without British hardware and textiles, and the overseas rum, sugar, tea, coffee, chocolate, and tobacco which passed through British hands, Europe defied him. Napoleon himself had to buy British greatcoats to equip his armies for the great Russian campaign.

All in all, the English and the Scots, from meager beginnings, responded more ably and industriously than other Europeans to the commercial opportunity created by ocean navigation. As that commerce grew, British domestic production grew with it—from the days when American bullion flowed through Spain to England because Spaniards could not or would not produce staple goods and had expelled on religious grounds the Moors and Jews who could, down to the time when the whole Continent was in considerable degree dependent on British exports.

By the end of the eighteenth century, Britain had taken some long and irrevocable strides towards industrialization, that is, the production on a large scale of manufactured goods. In the woolens trade, cloth production had become subdivided to an extraordinary degree in order to reap the fullest benefits of specialized skill. In cottons, where the competition of cheap hand labor in India had to be faced, a remarkable outburst of inventive genius about the middle of the century had produced man's first great battery of machinery. When this was perfected for spinning and weaving and adapted to the application of water power, modern industrial production began. Now not only was the British market no longer in need of tariff protection, but Britons could undersell Indian handicraft producers of cotton textiles in Indian as well as European and other markets.[13] A similar revolutionary development took place in hardware, when for the first time an inexpensive method of smelting iron ore with coal coke instead of charcoal was painfully worked out between 1708 and 1754 and supplemented by greatly improved processes for handling iron [14] and producing small quantities of steel.

All of these developments tended to draw machinery and workers together from cottage industry and the countryside to "mills" and towns near water power or to the remarkable districts where coal and iron could be mined not far apart. A new element entered the picture about 1769 when a young Scot, named James Watt, produced the first generally efficient steam engine. This he developed from a crude predecessor which had been invented by Thomas Newcomen at the beginning of the century for draining the deepening coal mines [15] and for producing the blast in iron furnaces. From about 1785 onwards, steam began to supplant water power.

Now a great interplay of old and new forces was under way. Markets, machines, heavy industry, mining, mechanical power, and improved transportation by land and water [16] were joined in a crescendo of efficient production which would steadily transform Britain and the world. The speed of this process has often been exaggerated. Factory production did not dominate British industry until about

[13] Thus stimulating American cotton production and the inventive skill of Eli Whitney in providing the cotton gin.

[14] Notably Henry Cort's puddling process and rolling mill of 1775–85.

[15] Humphrey Davy invented the safety lamp which facilitated deeper coal mining in 1815.

[16] The great Canal Age began about 1760, the McAdam-Telford road about 1800, the steam railway about 1825.

1850. Yet the immense industrial lead enjoyed by Great Britain, even before the French Revolution, goes far to explain the nation's strength during the Napoleonic wars.

It should be noted as well that British agriculture attained world pre-eminence during the eighteenth century, partly because of a great spurt in population which accompanied increased prosperity and better health,[17] and partly because men whose property was in land were pretty well driven to make it more productive in order to keep pace with the possessors of other forms of wealth. Progressive land managers introduced new crops, methods of cultivation, rotations, and fertilizers from other parts of Europe, notably the Low Countries, and combined them with native practice and much hard work in cultivation and drainage in order to bring new lands into bearing and make old lands yield as never before. The machine was made to serve agriculture in plowing, seeding, reaping, and threshing. In addition, systematic stock breeding was developed for the first time, partly by selective breeding of native strains for better wool, mutton, beef, and bacon, and partly by crossing with desirable imported stock.[18] The whole agricultural development was crowned by agricultural societies, fairs, and the publication of books and periodicals. Europe and America had begun to turn to Britain for agricultural improvement before the American and French revolutions took place.

It was not the least part of the genius of the younger Pitt that he devised the means whereby these great accretions of economic strength were harnessed to the political

[17] Plague disappeared and the newly discovered inoculation greatly reduced smallpox. The easily washable cotton shirt was more sanitary than its woolen predecessor.

[18] The Channel Islands, by their separation, almost automatically produced three distinct dairy strains, Jersey, Alderney, and Guernsey.

needs of the nation more efficiently than anywhere else in the world. During the 'eighties he consolidated the national debt and brought public obligations up to parity by sound financial practices. He instituted a sinking fund for redemption of the debt, took advantage of the revulsion against royal patronage to eliminate a lot of leakage of public money, simplified the national bookkeeping, and balanced the budget. Following Adam Smith's precepts, he reduced customs duties without seriously impairing the revenues, for the reductions diminished the crying scandal of smuggling. His weakness was a liking for excise taxes, a Dutch idea introduced by Parliament during the war with Charles I, and he saddled the British public with every imaginable form of this indirect taxation, originally on luxuries like carriages and servants, but ultimately on necessities like windows and ale. Against this can be balanced his success, early in the Napoleonic wars, in introducing the most equitable form of levy—the income tax.

In spite of all this prewar fiscal reform and the unique strength which it gave to British governments, the Revolutionary and Napoleonic wars could not be paid for by taxation, so that borrowing had to be resorted to. The national debt of about £240 million in 1784 rose to over £850 million in 1816. The pound was depreciated 25 per cent in Amsterdam, and public obligations had not only fallen far below parity, but had been issued at 30 or 40 per cent discount for years.

In other words, Great Britain had paid for her victory partly out of production and partly by inflation and, although no other country nearly approached her in financial and economic soundness, the coming of peace at once exposed the nation and its government to the necessity for immense readjustment and reconstruction. The propertied classes had prospered. The unpropertied had been driven down the slope of distress. For a generation reform and amelioration of all sorts had been repressed. Great Britain had battled through a struggle for survival to a victory of unforeseen magnitude. It remained to be seen whether her governors had the wit to realize that widespread reform was the only safety valve against a long overdue British Revolution.

CHAPTER VIII

The Victorian Gospel of Work
1815–1870

THE INSATIABLE appetites of over twenty years of war had inflated British agricultural and industrial production, and in 1815 both were suddenly faced by the collapse of government spending and by the inability of the prostrate Continent to buy. The mere burden of carrying the war debt was enough to require continued high taxation. The unemployment which came with peace was aggravated by the demobilization of hundreds of thousands of sailors and soldiers. The whole price structure, that is, everything from wages and prices to land values and mortgages, was tuned to a pound sterling which was no longer convertible into gold and which had fallen about a quarter below its former parity abroad.

The postwar misery of the laboring classes was appalling, for even during the full employment of the war period unscrupulous employers had taken advantage of the reactionary temper of the times to prevent labor from trying to improve its lot. Rural wages had been kept down; cottages had become scarce and had fallen into disrepair; and lands which farm laborers might have cultivated for themselves had been engulfed into new plowlands for the landlords.

Industry revealed all the evils which accompany a head-long rush into new and profitable enterprise. Nearly all factories were horrible places in which to work.[1] The machinery was dangerous; wages were low; hours were long; and the discovery that women and children could manage much of the machinery meant that male handicraftsmen were thrown into idleness while their wives and children were worked, sometimes literally, to death. Housing in the crowded new industrial centers was abominable.

Perhaps most serious of all was the fact that the very rapid increase of the population, both naturally and by immigration from Ireland, had brought Britain into a marginal position in the matter of self-support in food-stuffs. A bad harvest meant misery; a series of them meant semistarvation for many. Until the middle of the nine-teenth century crop shortages were invariably reflected in misery and unrest. The Reverend Robert Malthus had been much concerned by this question about 1797, and in a famous essay had drawn the melancholy conclusion that since population increased much faster than food production, there was nothing much to be done about the inevitable suffering except to recommend sexual continence as a better way of keeping down the population than disease and war. In the meantime, local magistrates were trying to keep the poor alive through a device invented by Berkshire justices in 1795 (the Speenhamland system), whereby wages were supplemented out of the poor rates in terms of the number of children a man had and the prevailing price of bread. This makeshift scheme pauperized and demoralized the poor and enabled employers to keep down wages, but it began to frighten those who had to pay local taxes, or "rates," when the postwar depression piled up its annual

[1] Robert Owen's New Lanark was a spectacular exception.

cost until in 1818 it amounted to 13s. 3d. per head of the population of England and Wales.[2]

The ups and downs of war had not entirely spared the heavily taxed propertied classes, particularly the speculators, unless they had the ability to turn paper profits into more stable forms of wealth. In particular, two problems of property demanded settlement in 1815. The landed interests wanted to maintain the inflated land values, rents, mortgages, etc., of the war period. They so dominated Parliament that they immediately passed a Corn Law which prohibited the importation of foreign grain until the domestic price had risen to a point which would support their price structure. Meanwhile the monied interests were holding £850,000,000 worth of national debt and, although they had acquired most of it at great discounts, they wanted to be repaid not only in full, but in gold pounds instead of paper. This group was less influential in Parliament than the landlords, who did not pretend to understand what was beginning to be called "political economy," but they got their way shortly after 1820. At the same time, the managers of the new industries were displaying remarkable, if ruthless, enterprise in trying to avoid bankruptcy. All sections of the propertied interest had combined to end the hated income tax in 1815, leaving the national revenue to depend chiefly on customs duties and endless heavy excises.

Having mended their own economic fences and condemned the unpropertied classes to bear an unfair proportion of the crushing burden of deflation, the majority of the ruling oligarchy conceived their job to be to sit on the lid of unrest until the underlying situation should improve.

---

[2] The total cost in 1818 was £8,000,000. Death by starvation was a formal category in British vital statistics until late in the nineteenth century.

Fortunately, however, there were some reformers who insisted on enjoying their ancient rights of free criticism in spite of the repressive legislation on the statute books, and who were relatively safe in doing so because they belonged to the upper classes or had influential friends there. Perhaps the most prominent group was composed of those Evangelical Anglicans and Nonconformists [3] who agitated for the abolition of slavery, prison reform, and other humanitarian causes. They came from both political parties, but tended to be Tories because their humanitarianism collided with harsh Whig economics in labor policies. The Tory, with the traditional sense of obligation towards dependents which had been a feature of feudal and manorial society, was outraged by what seemed to him the callousness of industrialists towards their workers. Even negro slavery, the Tories argued, implied an obligation which was contradicted when a factory shut down and left workers without wages, their only sustenance.

For various reasons, the Whig party tended to be the rallying ground for commerce, industry, and finance, but since it had been out of power for about fifty years and showed few signs of revival, a good many businessmen who wanted public influence had become Tories. They could afford to buy seats in the Commons. The result was that both old parties contained disturbing minorities of men who had seen the light of a new day in the dogmas of free trade and abolition of governmental interference with business which interested persons had built upon the writings of Adam Smith. These dogmas, reinforced by contributions from Malthus, James Mill, and David Ricardo, were being woven into the new faith of Laissez Faire—Hands Off Business. Its principles were elevated to the status of laws of

[3] The proportion of Quakers was notably high.

nature by the new businessmen and, because they insisted that such laws should not be broken merely on humanitarian grounds, economics quite properly earned its name of "the dismal science."

It was probably inevitable that the new industrial interest, faced by the task of making over the relationship between government and economics in Great Britain, should give its loyalty to sweeping new principles of an individualism in which the Devil was plainly to take the hindmost, but it made for a great deal of human misery after 1815. Moderation of that misery came chiefly from a curious alliance between humanitarian Tories and utilitarian Benthamites—a fortunate alliance too, because Tory common sense forced Benthamite "scientific" administration to keep its feet on the ground on numerous important occasions.

Yet there was little consistency about the expedient alliances which took shape among the reformers. In spite of the fact that the Laissez Faire group, or Manchester School, wanted to eliminate governmental regulation of economic enterprise, and that the Benthamite Utilitarians, or Westminster School, wanted government intervention in order to promote human happiness, the two schools had a confusing way of combining in order to shake up the lethargic majority of the governing oligarchy. Bentham himself was a good deal to blame, for in later life he diluted the purity of his early principles, apparently because he was so flattered to receive recognition from some of his own countrymen after twenty-five or thirty years of fame only among foreigners. It was Edwin Chadwick, a very late disciple of his, who gave Britons such a dose of Benthamite bureaucratic regulation that they cast him out of authority and never forgave him. The point to be made here is that in Parliament there was a small group of Benthamites, known

ADEN

ADEN

BAHAMAS

BARBADOS

BERMUDA

BASUTOLAND
BECHUANALAND
SWAZILAND

H.C.

BRITISH GUIANA

BRITISH HONDURAS

NEWFOUNDLAND

CEYLON

CYPRUS

FALKLAND IS.

FIJI IS.

Liam Dunne

GAMBIA

GIBRALTAR

GOLD COAST   GRENADA   HONG KONG   JAMAICA   KENYA   LEEWARD IS.

EX UNITATE VIRES
SOUTH AFRICA

ONWARD
NEW ZEALAND

GREENLAND

ALASKA

CANADA

UNITED
STATES

UNITED

EIRE

GIBRALTAR

BERMUDA

Bahama Is.

JAMAICA

LEEWARD IS.
BARBADOS
TRINIDAD

SOUTH
AMERICA

ASC

ST. HE

PITCAIRN

SAMOAN IS.

FALKLAND
IS.

FALKLAND
ISLANDS
DEPENDENCIES

THI

INDIA

BRITISH COMMONWEALTH
AND EMPIRE

SEPT. 1, 1939

as the Philosophical Radicals, each of whom had one or more pet schemes of reform, and most of whom could be counted upon to ally themselves with any groups which would pay for their votes by advancing their causes.

As the scarifying comments of the romantic poets Shelley and Byron testify, the last five years (1815–20) of George III's reign were horrible. The government was frankly afraid, and the Duke of Wellington knew only one way of dealing with such a situation, that is, repression by armed force. One section of the unprivileged population pinned its hopes almost entirely on political reform and set out to agitate for it in a perfectly proper way—the formation of public political societies and the holding of outdoor meetings. The successful growth of this movement was fatal, for in 1819 the authorities at Manchester completely lost their heads at the prospect of a demonstration in favor of universal suffrage and let loose the volunteer cavalry on the massed thousands in St. Peter's Fields. "Peterloo" became almost as famous as Waterloo when it was followed by a battery of temporary statutes which reduced the ordinary man's rights of expression to nothing.

During the next ten years—1820–30, the reign of the despicable George IV—the Tory governments continued to stamp out nearly all popular agitation, but sheer insistence on freezing things as they were weakened here and there at higher levels under the pressure of events. The ice jam was beginning to break. Thus George Canning, then Foreign Secretary, flatly refused to assist the other European powers in suppressing the revolutionary government which had been set up in Spain in 1820; and, when the Greeks revolted in 1821, not only did Britons and British money rally to their aid, but, when a Turkish fleet threatened to stifle the revolt in 1827, Great Britain organized a blockade with Russian and French aid which culminated in the destruction of the Turkish fleet at Navarino.

Similar encouragement to the widespread rebellions of Spanish colonies in the Americas furnishes a substantial clue to this line of behavior. Britain was eagerly seeking freer markets to engage the mighty productive apparatus which she had built up. She fought through and lost a wrangling struggle to keep the United States out of trade with the British West Indies. She dumped manufactures at the Battery in New York for what they might bring at auction. She poured goods, arms, soldiers, and sailors into any Latin-American country which welcomed them.

Gradually it became evident that the United States and Great Britain had substantial common interests in opening up as much as possible of Spanish America to their commerce. In fact, Canning had proposed in 1823 a joint Anglo-American declaration warning European nations not to intervene in the colonial revolutions, and, when John Adams and President Monroe proceeded to make the Monroe Doctrine a unilateral affair, he announced that Britain would fight any effort to recover the Spanish colonies. His words carried more weight than Monroe's because they had the British navy behind them. He told the Commons: "I called the New World into existence to redress the balance of the Old."

Events at home showed an equal determination to open up the channels of world trade by getting rid of the mercantilistic regulations against which Adam Smith had argued so persuasively. Britain's pioneering productive advantage over the rest of the world made it good economic nationalism for her to embark on free trade; but she was sorely handicapped in this effort by her needs for revenue from customs duties to help carry her indebtedness. During the 'twenties, therefore, Frederick Robinson (Chancellor of the Exchequer) and William Huskisson (President of the Board of Trade) worked chiefly to survey the tariff structure and mercantilistic regulations, cutting out dead wood here, reducing duties wherever practicable, and in general simplifying an encrusted mass into such form that reciprocal trade treaties might be made more easily and the whole tariff level be reduced at any time that an improved fiscal position made it possible. They did not want to shift the burden to hateful excises and they rightly believed that lowered duties would increase the volume of trade sufficiently to offset decrease in revenue.

The 'twenties yielded some other improvements. Prison reform made substantial advances, and a Benthamite campaign for reform of the penal law found its way down through the hands of Sir Samuel Romilly and Sir James Mackintosh to Sir Robert Peel, who crowned their work by getting rid of the death penalty for about a hundred offenses. Trade unions were legalized again in 1824 and 1825,[4] and in 1828 and 1829 the repeal of the Test and Corporation acts and Catholic Emancipation restored the rights of citizenship to non-Anglicans. Thus Ireland at last secured a direct and reasonably representative voice in the United Kingdom Parliament.

The inadequacy and slow effects of these Tory reforms became apparent when the 'twenties ended with Britain on the brink of revolution. The Whigs responded to the situation by reviving their ancient cause of Parliamentary reform and, temporarily at least, most of the reformers swung in behind them in order to force Parliament to re-

---

[4] An achievement of the Benthamite tailor, Francis Place, who professed to believe that once trade unions were legal they would be found unnecessary.

model itself and thereby become more truly representative of, and responsive to, national demands. In effect, the
owners of new forms of property, well aware that they had
been represented badly or not at all, saw their chance to
force the landed oligarchy to make room for them in the
seats of government by recruiting in a threatening alliance
almost the whole volume of discontent. For two hectic years
(1830–32) the Tory citadel was besieged by a motley army
of forces which ranged from quite conservative Whigs, who
merely wanted to supplant the Tories, to downright democratic republicans who wanted to upset the entire apple
cart. Surrender came in the Reform Act of 1832 which
transferred over one hundred and forty indefensibly unrepresentative seats to more populous areas and broadened
the franchise.

Democracy had first stormed the American national
government in 1825 when Andrew Jackson and his friends
"took over" Washington, but Great Britain was to lag
behind for another generation. The Reform Act of 1832,
while it increased the electorate by 40 per cent, actually
disenfranchised large numbers of voters in the few democratic "scot and lot" boroughs where all ratepayers had
hitherto had votes. The act was a middle-class triumph,
and the democrats were promptly informed by "Finality
Jack" Russell of the Whig right wing that the progressive
ideas of "Radical Jack" Lambton [5] of the tiny left wing
were out of the question. Thus the great mass of the people,
whose impressive agitation had won victory for the Whigs
by frightening the House of Lords into surrender, was condemned to wait patiently for whatever improvements the
new masters of the United Kingdom might be pleased to

[5] Baron, and later Earl of, Durham. He had been closely associated with
Lord John Russell in pushing through the Reform Act.

concede. Apparently the greatest anxiety of the Whigs was to persuade the Tories that there was nothing revolutionary or democratic about them.

The reforms which followed during the 'thirties and 'forties were middle-class reforms except in a few instances where Benthamite interventionism formed an effective alliance with Tory humanitarianism.[6] Thus in 1833 slavery was finally abolished in all British territories and the owners of nearly a million slaves were compensated. In the same year, the first effective Factory Act was passed, initiating a cumulative process which has gone on ever since.[7] It abolished the employment of children under nine, except in silk mills, and limited women's working day to ten hours, with considerable effect on the related working day of men.[8] It foreshadowed the future by establishing a central authority and traveling inspectors with powers of magistrates.

In 1834 the much-amended Elizabethan Poor Laws and the Speenhamland system were shelved in favor of a new Poor Law along Benthamite lines. This emerged from an odd alliance of the Westminster and Manchester schools and was so inelastic and inhumane that it aroused sufficient Tory and popular resistance to ensure its partial failure. It attempted to abolish all relief outside workhouses and at the same time to keep workhouse relief at a level which would make it less desirable than employment outside, a

[6] The Benthamite bureaucrat, Edwin Chadwick, took an active, often a decisive, part in guiding the following reforms: poor law, factory legislation, police, and public health. His principal Tory associate was Lord Ashley (after 1851 the Earl of Shaftesbury), whose activities extended also to a large variety of philanthropic enterprises at home and abroad.

[7] Acts of 1802 and 1819 had meant well, but failed for lack of powers of enforcement.

[8] Hours of work for children nine to twelve years old were nine, and for those thirteen to eighteen were thirteen and a half.

principle which has persisted in some degree in English-speaking countries down to our own time. In 1835 a large number of municipal corporations were placed under elective councils, thus extending political reform into the field of local government, and in 1839 police systems similar to the one then recently devised for Metropolitan London were authorized for the rest of England and Wales on a county basis.

Obviously the reforms of the 'thirties, except perhaps for the Factory Act and some temporary effects of Parliamentary reform, cannot have greatly diminished the revolutionary energies which were generated by popular distress and which came to a head whenever the fatal combination of bad harvests and the Corn Law raised the price of bread. Probably, therefore, the explanation why Great Britain did not have a revolution during the first half of the nineteenth century must be found in the large demand for unskilled labor which was fairly continuously sustained by expansion in road, canal, and railway building and in other construction.[9]

George Stephenson's successful steam locomotive of 1825 transformed rail travel from horses and short hauls into the basic long- and short-haul system of transportation, for the next century at least. The number of man-hours which went into satisfying the immediate "mania" for railway construction was the great safety valve for popular unrest during the next generation. In Great Britain, the railways were from the beginning constructed with more expense and more concern for the public than elsewhere in the world, so that their thousands of miles of carefully finished cuttings and embankments absorbed perhaps three or four

[9] Large-scale emigration, partly to British colonies, but chiefly to the United States, also eased the pressure.

times as much human labor as the same extent of railroad required in the United States.

It seems significant that the next outburst of popular agitation came after the speculative collapse and "Panic" of 1837, when railway building was at least as hard hit as other enterprises. This was the ardent agitation in favor of the People's Charter, a petition to Parliament drawn up in the form of a bill whose enactment would secure universal suffrage, the secret ballot, equal constituencies, abolition of property qualifications for Members of Parliament, salaries for them, and annual Parliaments.

The movement began in London and spread rapidly over the nation, enlisting enthusiastic working-class support, but when the House of Commons rejected the petition, its supporters broke up into warring factions. An attempted general strike failed for lack of funds, the South favored persuasion, and the North threatened physical force. A feeble attempt to release a Chartist from jail in Wales provoked the troops to fire and was followed by ruthless punishment of the respectable leader, John Frost. A second monster petition was rejected by the Commons in 1842. The third and largest, presented while thousands of troops and special constables stood by to prevent Britain from joining the rest of Europe in revolution in 1848, met the same fate and the movement was diffused into other channels in the mid-'fifties.

The failure of this great democratic cause has been, with some justice, ascribed to the inability of the ill-educated working classes to throw up able and determined leaders. A shrewder view of the "Hungry 'Forties," however, would perceive that labor had not yet shaken off its reliance on the middle class for support and for some degree of guidance. This was demonstrated when the middle class paralleled Chartism by pouring much money and energy into a great and popular campaign against the Corn Laws which drew off many workers into a vivid, exciting, and successful campaign for repeal.

The circumstance which finally, in 1846, made it impossible for the landed interest any longer to maintain the duties on imported grain was the tragic famine which devastated Ireland when the potato, its greatest food crop, was destroyed by an incurable blight.[10] Yet before that happened, two textile manufacturers, Richard Cobden and John Bright, had persuaded both their own class and many workers that immense benefits (lower wages, but cheaper bread) would follow the extension of free trade principles to basic foodstuffs even if it meant the death of British agriculture through American competition.[11]

In addition to repeal of the Corn Laws, the Mines Act of 1842 and the so-called Ten Hours Act of 1847, towards which Lord Ashley had devoted his energies, eased the lot of miners and factory workers, and cholera epidemics frightened the upper classes into giving some support to the campaign for public health authority which Chadwick and his friend Dr. Southwood Smith had been conducting for twenty years with slowly increasing success. Whatever the motives behind it, British paternalism could still anticipate and thwart democracy.

By the time that Britain passed the great revolutionary year, 1848, without an outbreak, the painful recuperation and readjustments after the Napoleonic wars were over, and leadership in the industrial revolution was about to yield obvious dividends even to the working classes. In 1851,

10 "Rotten potatoes have done it," said Wellington, "they put Peel in his damned fright."

11 A series of wars abroad saved British agriculture until the late 'seventies.

the nation celebrated its achievement by an unparalleled exhibition in London. Here under the patronage of the now popular Queen Victoria [12] and her German Prince Consort, Albert, who was systematically kept in his place by the governing classes, the marvels of British industry were garishly displayed. Ingenuity and enterprise were more conspicuous than good taste, but only the inventive Americans and the cultivated French could have faintly rivaled this great revelation of Britain's achievements. The enormous Crystal Palace which enclosed tall trees and gardens may have been vulgar, but the world admitted that it was magnificent and tried to imitate it. [13]

During the 'fifties and 'sixties, most Britons, from the top of society to the bottom, subscribed to the Victorian gospels of work and respectability, largely because prosperity seemed to flow from them. Free trade, Laissez Faire, peace, thrift, good national bookkeeping, and gradual paternalistic reform seemed justified by their works. The national government became something like a large business. Waste and sinecures were resolutely attacked; the Civil Service was reformed by the gradual introduction of competitive examinations; and the two great Parliamentarians of the time, Benjamin Disraeli and W. E. Gladstone, embarked on their long public duel in behalf of the Conservative and Liberal parties, respectively, by matching skills in planning and defending the annual budget. [14] The Liberal slogan, "Peace, Retrenchment, and Reform," com-

[12] She had succeeded to the Crown in 1837 at the age of eighteen, married in 1840, and had given "Victorianism" its tone by her large family and extreme respectability.

[13] The sparrows which also got enclosed presented a problem which the Queen put up to Wellington. He recommended sparrow hawks.

[14] They both owed much to Peel, particularly for his courage in reintroducing the income tax in 1842, but Disraeli won his leadership by attacking Peel for the "great betrayal" of repeal of the Corn Laws.

prised a combination which it was hard for Britons to resist.

Once the privations and hard work of the period from 1815 to 1850 were past, British wealth began to pile up at an awe-inspiring rate. Gold discoveries in California and Australia assisted, about 1850, in arresting a depressing decline in world prices, and the upward turn stimulated business. British railway-builders, engineers, and industrialists, who had burned their fingers rather badly in earlier enterprises abroad, now began to find highly profitable employment for their capital and skills on the Continent, in the Americas, in India, and in Australasia. Domestic industry, firm on its foundations of coal, iron, and textiles, expanded at a rapid rate to meet the demands of home consumption and of a foreign trade unrivaled by any other nation.[15]

The working classes were so much better off that foreigners noted with amazement that members of its upper layers wore the same kind of clothes as gentlemen did. The trade-union movement had made impressive strides among highly skilled workmen, so much so that the "big" or "amalgamated" unions were becoming very cautious about risking their well-invested funds in strikes, and were inclined to be rather critical of the less substantial associations of more poorly paid labor. The miners, for instance, were regarded almost as a subhuman species. In mid-Victorian times, "from rags to riches" had a widespread appeal. The irresistible allure of petty capitalism ruined all attempts at producers' co-operatives at the same time that consumers' co-operatives were flourishing.

A society "on the make," where standards of material success are omnipresent, has a way of discouraging un-

---

[15] It jumped from about £80 million in 1820 to about £550 million in 1870. Most of it, and a great deal of non-British commerce, was carried in British ships.

worldly artistic endeavor. Britain paid for two generations of narrow concentration on mechanical ingenuity by the decline of the arts. Good taste was driven underground. The rich promise of the Romantic Movement which had produced so much memorable, enduring poetry and prose at the beginning of the nineteenth century faded out into insignificance.[16] British music, painting, sculpture, and architecture descended into puffed-up vulgarity and imitativeness. Dramatists labored in vain to breathe life into hack work. A man of great poetic gifts, like Tennyson, overshadowed his finest achievements by stooping to contemporary expectations, or like Browning, by escaping either into obscurity or into shallow, hearty optimism.

Only in fiction were the prevailing standards notably high. Jane Austen (1775–1817) had surpassed Scott by her cool and penetrating revelations of the human comedy, and the Brontë sisters and George Eliot maintained the position which she had made for women authors, although in different fashions.[17] Dickens and Thackeray, however, were the great novelists of the English-speaking world from about 1835 until long after their deaths. Vessels raced across the Atlantic to deliver fresh installments of their works, and both men faced their admirers in lectures and readings in the United States and Canada.

Yet in the gallery of world literature these men have not been conceded first rank, largely, it would appear, because they dared not offend the public by complete sincerity. Dickens laid a covering of sentimentality over his rich revelations of lower-class and lower middle-class life, and Thackeray betrayed both his clear vision of the materialism

16 Wordsworth, Scott, Coleridge, Byron, Shelley, and Keats spent their forces between 1798 and about 1825.

17 Charlotte, Emily, and Anne Brontë, and Mary Ann Evans, whose pseudonym was George Eliot.

which pervaded Britain between 1815 and 1860 and his own gifts of wit and humor by a pseudocynical satirical style and by prudery. The mid-Victorian era was congenial chiefly to morally earnest essayists: whether Thomas Carlyle, with his reverberating Jeremiads in behalf of natural aristocracy and responsible paternalism; or T. B. Macaulay, with his brilliant assurances that the British genius had hit its proper stride in conquest of the material world; or the confused, if eloquent, art critic and social reformer, John Ruskin.

The world figure of the time in Great Britain was an invalid naturalist, Charles Darwin.[18] After several years of field work in and near South America, and more of study, classification, and comparison at home, he was induced by loyal friends to publish in 1859 a book entitled *On the Origin of Species by Means of Natural Selection, or the Preservation of Favoured Races in the Struggle for Life.* It is not too much to say that this volume, presenting disturbing conceptions which Darwin had formed fifteen or twenty years earlier, caused a world-wide revolution in man's ideas of his nature and of his place in the universe.

Darwin had drawn together the findings of geology, zoology, and botany, together with the current speculations concerning biological evolution,[19] and now presented, with whole batteries of corroboration from nature, a hypothesis which hinged on a phrase of Malthus—"the struggle for existence." He made it seem probable that all forms of animal life, including man, had developed out of earlier, primi-

[18] The more profound genius of James Clerk Maxwell (1831–79) was known only to a small number of men in the world who glimpsed the fundamental importance of his deep insights into the nature of matter and of energy and the mathematical relationships applicable to them.

[19] His grandfather Erasmus Darwin had been a picturesque writer in this field.

tive forms. The repercussions in theology, philosophy, and science itself were tremendous and prolonged. As these were diffused into general British habits of thought, they had two profound effects. One was that survival tended to become an ultimate value, or determinant of behavior. The other was that Darwinian evolution was fairly rapidly blended with Victorian optimism to form a belief in progress, that is, a belief that nearly all change was for the better.

It was natural that with so much profitable enterprise going on at home, Britons should have been relatively oblivious to what was happening elsewhere. To this attitude, in part, can be attributed the resolute anti-imperialism which prevailed from about 1840 to about 1870. This so-called Little Englandism was a natural accompaniment of Laissez Faire and free trade. After the American Revolution there had been a noticeable disinclination to acquire territory overseas except small bases which might be useful for commerce or for naval strategy. The triumph of free trade transformed this mood into a widespread belief that the colonies would trade with Great Britain anyway and that expenditures for their maintenance and defense were a sheer waste of money. In particular, the "scientific" colonization and assisted emigration to Australia and New Zealand promoted by E. G. Wakefield were found both uneconomical and of little effect in diminishing population pressure in the British Isles. The wars against the Maoris in New Zealand, which lasted until 1864, it was felt, ought to be the responsibility of New Zealanders themselves.

British statesmen came to believe that colonies like the North American and Australasian ones should be expected to mature and to stand on their own feet. This belief was natural enough in Manchesterites like Cobden and Bright, but even the Conservative leader Disraeli described the colonies as "a millstone round our necks." The anti-imperialistic attitude was reflected in not very success-ful efforts to grapple with the deep-lying problems of Ire-land; the surrender to Canadian demands for self-govern-ment, and the extension of the same right to similar colo-nies elsewhere; and the last step in obliterating the old mercantilistic system of empire by the repeal of the Navi-gation Acts in 1849. This thoroughgoing about-face hit the economic organization of the North American colonies very hard, but the assumption in Great Britain was that they were bound to join the United States sooner or later anyway.

The great exception to this anti-imperialistic policy was India. Here the British population was minute in spite of the territorial expansion which had gone on unceasingly after the days of Dupleix and Clive and had been acceler-ated by French intrigue in the days of Napoleon. Most of the Indian peninsula was under direct or indirect British control by 1825 and an even-handed, if expensive, British administration made rapid and widespread improvement in the living conditions of those Indians who lived within the British Raj, or area of direct rule. It was not to be ex-pected that the British administration at home or in India could conceive of restoring Indian independence and thus hazarding the improvements and the profitable investments which accompanied British rule. Looking back on the Indian chaos of the eighteenth century, Britons acquired a reassuring sense of their civilizing mission in India; and Indians, while quite naturally regarding them as conquer-ors, admitted that there were compensations for their con-quered state in the unaccustomed order and justice and in the material improvements which accompanied British rule.

The great threat to India in British eyes was no longer France, but rapidly expanding Russia, whether in Afghanistan to the northwest, or in the threatened domination of Turkey, which controlled the short route to India by way of the eastern Mediterranean. Herein lay the explanation of the Crimean War which Britain fought against Russia in alliance with France and Turkey from 1854 to 1856. It proved a shocking revelation of the depths to which British armed strength had fallen during forty years of peace, an impression which was confirmed in 1857 when stupid, rather than malevolent, treatment of the Sepoys, or native troops in India, provoked a serious mutiny there. That outbreak ended the East India Company. Henceforth Parliament assumed complete responsibility for the government of India.

British policy towards China underlines the difference in British thinking about colonies of European stock like Canada and New Zealand and about areas of commercial enterprise and investment among non-Europeans like India. The proud Chinese looked down on all foreigners and segregated their commercial agents in the vicinity of Canton. Here, by using Indian opium for exchange in spite of official Chinese prohibition, the East India Company built up a great advantage over its principal competitors, the Americans. While there were extenuating circumstances arising out of Chinese graft and piracy and out of the intense, unprincipled competition among the foreign merchants, perhaps the most shameful incidents in British imperialism were the Opium Wars of 1840–42 and of 1858–60, by which Britain and France forced China to accept in trade the drug which was debauching her people. Britons at home knew little about all this, but in response to the demands of overseas interests British governments sent out the naval and military expeditions which China could not withstand.[20]

Those governments were not yet truly representative of the British people, for Parliament kept finding other things to do after 1850 when extension of the franchise was proposed, and it was not until 1867 that the copestone of political democracy topped off the achievement of world leadership. When it came, this decision to grant the vote to male urban workers seemed to be merely an ultraclever play by Disraeli in the course of a fascinating contest with Gladstone for leadership of Parliament and the nation, but it was truly the product of deeper forces. Thanks to increased prosperity and to a higher price level, about twice as many persons had been automatically enfranchised by attaining the necessary property qualifications between 1832 and 1865 as had been added to the voter's lists at the time of the Act of 1832. Thus the lower middle class was progressively getting the vote, and men like John Bright developed the belief that it might advantageously be extended still lower.

Labor was well organized and had able leaders. The behavior of the suffering textile workers when cotton supplies were cut off by the American Civil War had been so admirable that the common man simply had to be included among the defenders of Victorian decency and propriety. All the democratic aspirations of three generations of lowly people had become focused in one confident and impressive demand for the vote, that is, for recognition as Britons. That demand could not with safety have been denied, and, while Disraeli's "leap in the dark" may have bewildered his own party and "dished the Whigs," it was little more

[20] The East India Company's monopoly had ended in 1833. Hong Kong was ceded in 1842 and other ports were opened.

than a proper diagnosis of a situation which most of his class could not estimate.

In these circumstances, it is some measure of Thomas Carlyle's inadequacy as a prophet for his own people that the concession of democracy, the inclusion in the active body politic of the masses whose energies had made possible the Victorian achievement, aroused him to an angry diatribe entitled "Shooting Niagara." The embittered old Scotsman could not see that, temporarily at least, the majority of British manhood belonged in one political tabernacle because its members worshiped the same set of rather materialistic Victorian gods, or that, even in terms of his own gospel of work, the laborer was worthy of his hire.

CHAPTER IX

Responses to Rivalry
1870–1918

In 1871, two things happened which were to be followed by far-reaching consequences for Great Britain. In the first place, a German federation, led and dominated by Prussia, topped off successful wars against Denmark and Austria by crushing France in six months and proclaiming the King of Prussia German Emperor. This long-delayed unification of German aptitudes, resources, and man power created a contender for European and world leadership with which Britons were to fail to come to terms. In the second place, by the Treaty of Washington, the Gladstone government admitted to the powerful United States which had emerged after the Civil War that an earlier Whig government had been wrong in permitting the *Alabama* and other Confederate commerce raiders to escape from British ports, and agreed to submit the question of damage claims to arbitration. The swallowing of this bitter pill laid the foundations of a durable Anglo-American understanding.

For various reasons, the Germans had not enjoyed a leading position in Europe since the Middle Ages, and they had had to fight through to national unity by accepting harsh Prussian direction instead of easy-going Austrian suzerainty. The whole achievement had taken over two centuries and had required a large amount of war, suffering, and disciplined organization. Their new nation was rich in little except military prestige, man power, ambition, respect for learning, scientific achievement, and a notable heritage of philosophy and music. Yet, like the Japanese a generation later, they saw a golden opportunity if they could on the one hand maintain or increase their armed preeminence and on the other set up an industrial establishment of the most advanced type under high tariff protection.[1] With little antiquated equipment to hamper them, and with confirmed habits of hard work, they might profitably invade European and world markets. Then the young athlete could elbow aside the old hands and secure "a place in the sun."

Britain's relationship with the United States was a different matter, for although there was no other such well-endowed nation under the sun except Russia, the American people still had almost half of their own area to exploit and their industrial production was far more for home consumption than for the world market. The United States needed British capital and access to the British market for its cotton, wheat, and tobacco so badly that, in spite of a narrowing American market for British goods, the economic relationship seemed bound to be mutually beneficial. Certain territorial and commercial rivalries between the two countries did exist throughout the Americas, in the Pacific, and in the Far East, but the Treaty of Washington was a promising mutual renewal of an earlier willingness to settle differences by discussion and concessions instead of by force.[2]

[1] The indemnity exacted from France was used to finance the purchase and construction of industrial equipment.

[2] Jay's Treaty of 1794 concerning the settlement of North American problems, which is regarded as the cornerstone of modern international arbitra-

It was too much to expect that the relationship of the two peoples could be instinctively cordial, in spite of the millions of Britons who continued to pour westward across the Atlantic. The tradition of the Revolution and of the War of 1812 persisted and it was constantly reinforced by the bitter feelings towards England of the American Irish. The Civil War itself had been a crucial strain, for the upper classes of an England which was still aristocratically governed had in the beginning preferred Southern oligarchy to Northern democracy, and the British textile industry had been starved for want of Southern cotton. When Lincoln emphatically declared that the war was for preservation of the Union rather than for abolition of slavery, Britons, with forty years of encouragement to "subject nationalities" like the Greeks and the Spanish Americans behind them, felt that the South deserved sympathy and support.

The masses of the population, however, straining for democracy themselves, had overwhelmingly aligned themselves with the North, and when the President issued the Emancipation Proclamation, the upper classes remembered Britain's own honorable extinction of slavery. John Bright and other liberal democrats were able to reach the White House through American friends with useful effects on both sides of the Atlantic. By the time the war ended, the "Alabama Claims" were the only great barrier to resumption of relatively amicable Anglo-American relations.

By means of what J. B. Moore, a leading American authority on international law, in 1937 called "the greatest treaty of actual and immediate arbitration the world has ever seen," all of the problems involving Great Britain and

tion, had set a precedent for the Treaty of Ghent after the War of 1812, but the subsequent extravagances of American "Manifest Destiny" had pushed the idea into the background.

the United States, including some stubborn difficulties relating to territory, fisheries, and trade which affected the new Dominion of Canada,[3] were settled between 1871 and 1877. Great Britain paid $15,500,000 for the Alabama Claims and the United States paid $5,500,000 for her use of the inshore North Atlantic fisheries. Inevitably there were some hard feelings and uncandid behavior on both sides, but it was an amazing achievement. Thanks to the skill of the Canadian Prime Minister, Sir John A. Macdonald, the young dominion, which had rightly expected to be a burnt-offering to agreement between the major parties, came out of the melee reasonably well. Not least of her good fortune was that the United States accepted her transcontinental expanse as a boundary to ebullient Manifest Destiny.

In 1873, the world economy was shaken by a severe depression and widespread dislocation. As the worst shocks passed away, Britons began to feel that their own economy had lost some of its expansive vigor. As recently as 1860, when Cobden had persuaded the French to try the effects of lowering tariff barriers, optimistic Britons had expected the world to follow them into free trade, but now the very opposite was happening. During and after the Civil War, the United States frankly adopted protectionism, and nearly all other countries, even most of Britain's self-governing colonies, followed the same course. These tariffs aimed at more than providing national revenues. It was plain that every state which could do so was going to build high fences behind which it could try out the British industrial formula for getting rich.

[3] This federation of the British North American colonies had been founded in 1867 and had extended itself to the Pacific by 1871, largely because such an association seemed the only possible protection against vigorous American annexationism.

This change in the world's economic climate coincided with a gradual revival of imperialism in Great Britain. Attempts have been made to explain this about-face from Little Englandism in terms of such single causes as Disraeli's shrewdness or Sir John Seeley's infectious lectures on the expansion of England. On the economic side, it has been pointed out that as the returns on domestic enterprise and investment declined from their early high levels, and as British skill in world banking increased, there had been a marked tendency to export railway, industrial, and engineering materials and to lend the money required to pay for them. The volume of this movement in 1872 was the highest in history and was not to be equaled for thirty years, and there is abundant evidence that in some circles there were rosy dreams of the rewards of enterprise overseas. Yet the flag did not necessarily follow the funds. British governments had for two generations refused to protect foreign investments by force, thereby establishing a convention.[4] In addition, most of the foreign investment was in the United States, Latin America, or other regions, where there was no idea of acquiring new territory.

The most reasonable general explanation of the imperialistic revival in Great Britain seems to be the rapid development of a great international competition when other countries tried to catch up in the race which Britons had led since 1763. For example, a French syndicate completed the Suez Canal in 1869, thus revolutionizing communications with India and the Far East. Consequently, when in 1875 the bankrupt Khedive of Egypt wanted to sell his Suez shares, Disraeli, without consulting Parliament, bor-

---

[4] Suppression of rebellion against existing British authority, as in Canada or India, excepted. The convention was first seriously impaired in 1877 in connection with Egypt.

rowed the money to buy them for Great Britain. Parliament approved the *coup* and also the colorful gesture which followed two years later—assumption of the title "Empress of India" by Queen Victoria.[5] At about the same time, Russia was expanding through Central Asia towards India, and, shaking off the shackles placed on her naval power in the Black Sea after the Crimean War, seemed about to overwhelm the Balkans and Turkey and become a Mediterranean power. Disraeli sent armies to bring Afghanistan back under British direction, and suceeeded in upsetting the peace terms imposed by Russia upon Turkey in 1878, replacing them with a new settlement by a congress of powers at Berlin which bolstered up Turkey and balanced Austria against Russia.[6]

So it went and so it was to go in various parts of the world until the British conscience finally rebelled against the disgrace of the South African War at the turn of the century. Queen Victoria's two Jubilees, in 1887 and 1897, with their colorful display of colonial armed forces, strange potentates, and delegations from all corners of the earth, were symbols of a heady imperialism which needed a deeper sense of responsibility, if only for its own good. Even Gladstone, who in 1880 fought and defeated Disraeli on the imperialist issue in Britain's first all-out popular election,[7] failed in his efforts to stem the tide. He might blame mis-

[5] She had mourned Prince Albert after his death in 1861 with such relentless thoroughness and retirement that she had fallen out of favor. There was even an avowed republican movement in Parliament and the nation early in the 'seventies. Disraeli succeeded in coaxing her out into a career of pageantry after 1877 which contributed enormously to the symbolic function of succeeding monarchs.

[6] He also pocketed Cyprus as an additional protection for Suez.

[7] The seventy-year-old Liberal shocked the Queen and old-line politicians by going directly to the people in a lively speaking tour. Popular response, contrasted with upper-class coldness, converted Gladstone into a believer in democracy.

sionaries, bankers, merchants, soldiers, or sailors, but he
could not prevent conscious and unconscious British empire builders from trying to keep ahead of six or eight
determined competitors. The rivalry for territory, raw
materials, and markets was intense, particularly in Africa,
and was frequently carried on by almost uncontrollable
private agents in the field. In the circumstances, it is to
Gladstone's credit that he focused his last energies [8] (and
destroyed his political party) in a stubborn attempt to
rectify Britain's oldest and worst imperial failure by granting Home Rule to Ireland. In spite of, or perhaps because
of, the clever and determined activities of Irish nationalists,
he failed.

From the Panic of 1873 to 1896, when world prices
turned upwards and "prosperity" returned, the propertied
classes in Britain "lived rich and talked poor." Actually,
in terms of real increases in national wealth, income of
employed persons, and average output per head, Great
Britain went ahead faster during the so-called Great Depression of 1873–96 than during the so-called Great Boom
of 1896–1913, but almost everyone firmly believed the opposite until students of the Depression of 1930 uncovered
the facts of the earlier period. The explanations for the
gloom and concern during the last quarter of the nineteenth century seem to be that foreign competition somewhat unnerved Britons who had had everything their own
way for two generations; that falling prices were most
misleadingly confused with declining prosperity; and that
there were repeated periods of extensive unemployment.[9]
In addition, the effects on the domestic economy of a

---

[8] His seventy-eighth to eighty-fifth years.

[9] The *Oxford English Dictionary* dates the term, "the unemployed," from
1882.

cumulative shift to overseas enterprise were imperfectly understood, and the belated advent of democracy in politics and in trade unionism after 1867 made the troubles and the activities of the masses more prominent and dramatic than they had ever been before.

For the propertied classes the Gospel of Work gave way to the Gospel of Leisure. Family businesses became limited companies, immense amalgamations were formed, and a great deal of the national wealth was represented by bonds and stocks whose dividends supported what was relatively the largest leisured class in the world. The British aristocracy, unlike its Spanish and French predecessors because of its single line of descent, continued to recruit new blood and new wealth by creations of nobility and marriages among the upper middle class.[10]

The "milord anglais" of 1700 to 1830 was succeeded by a new type, the gentleman amateur, or "sportsman." The cult of competitive games played for their own sakes and for moral as well as physical advantages had flowered into a national code from its modest beginnings under Arnold at Rugby School and from the "muscular Christians" who had been coming out of Oxford and Cambridge since the 'forties. Sportsmanship reinforced the older humanitarianism. Even women were rebelling against being merely stupid and good and were trying to be Christian Socialists in scores of philanthropic organizations. Many sins can be laid at the doors of Late Victorian wealth, but it had two consciences which saved it from complete social callousness—the ancient landlord's notion of *noblesse oblige* and the Christian injunctions to charity which tempered the harsh individualism of the businessman's ethics. The "settlement house" in the slums was a new symbol.

[10] Alliances with American heiresses began to be made more frequently.

The great issue, of course, was whether social welfare should be a voluntary concession from the propertied classes or a conquest by the unpropertied, and the last quarter of the nineteenth century was a crucial period in this unending contest. Conservative and Liberal leaders competed from 1866 onwards in dragooning their less alert Parliamentary followers into all kinds of social legislation—public education, factory acts, protection of trade unions, provisions for public health and housing, more efficient and democratic local government, and so on. Progressive municipalities vied with one another in creating public wealth, whether in the form of schools, libraries, art galleries, and parks, or water works, street railways, gas works, and harbor construction. In Birmingham this movement threw up a much feared "Radical," or "Republican," businessman in Joseph Chamberlain, the "gas and water Socialist," who provided Britain with its first efficient machine politics in the course of his rise to the mayoralty.[11] When he progressed to Parliament as John Bright's colleague in 1876, he injected into national politics both his radicalism and his system of getting out the vote. He and his political manager, Francis Schnadhorst, played a large part in Gladstone's resounding defeat of Disraeli in 1880.

Meanwhile Labor was accommodating itself to democracy, both in relation to the national parliament and to its own parliament, the Trade Union Congress. For the time being, it threw its political votes to Liberals or Conservatives in return for promises of this or that reform, but within the Congress the old leaders of the highly skilled workers found it difficult to adjust themselves to the pressure of numbers and votes from the large miners' unions and from

---

[11] The family fortune was based upon an American invention in screw making which had come to British notice at the Exhibition of 1851.

other large associations of the unskilled or semiskilled. Whatever the underlying increase in national prosperity, there were periods of disastrous unemployment for the masses and strikes, like those of the Dockworkers and the Match Girls, which stirred the public conscience.[12] In the face of such distress, the old trade-union oligarchy fought a losing fight against the New Unionism of numbers. Until that issue was settled, however, Labor could not bring any concentrated energy directly to bear upon national politics.

It is often forgotten that Karl Marx and his indispensable supporter Friedrich Engels spent the most productive part of their lives in England, and that Marx drew most of the factual material for *Das Kapital* from the records of the industrialization of Great Britain. Yet Britons repeatedly disappointed the two German socialists by failing to take the leading role in world revolution. In fact, British labor leaders showed a most exasperating fatherly condescension towards the many kinds of political refugees from the Continent who made London their haven from persecution. The British workman, because of tradition and other forces which did not fit into Marxian calculations, was both a gradualist and a believer in the political rather than the revolutionary approach to change. He was likely to be more concerned about teaching British ways to the thousands of Continental immigrants who were entering the labor market than receptive to the teachings of foreign political and economic theorists.[13]

Marx's ideas simply did not take hold in England as they did elsewhere in Europe. They were merely one element

---

[12] Unemployment among Trade Unionists was over 5 per cent from 1877 to 1880, 1884 to 1888, and 1892 to 1895. The percentage would be higher for the unorganized.

[13] London was a safe refuge for Continental socialists, communists, anarchists, and nihilists.

in a ferment of minority causes during the 'eighties and 'nineties, and almost no one studied them thoroughly, probably because most of *Das Kapital* remained in a language which few Britons could read. Marxism did little more than color, in diminishing degree, the socialist creeds of the little groups in H. M. Hyndman's Social Democratic Federation, William Morris's Socialist League, and the gradualist Fabian Society.[14] British socialism was a delicate plant cultivated by members of the middle class; it was humanitarian rather than systematic; and it made a good deal less of an impression on the population than the single-tax ideas of the American, Henry George.

The inimitable team of Gilbert and Sullivan [15] reflected in burlesque all of the foibles and ferments of this transitional period. Beginning with *Trial by Jury,* a satire on English law, in 1875, and ending (after a disagreement) with *The Gondoliers,* a satire on English democracy, in 1889, they held up to ridicule old institutions and panaceas for their reform. Parliament and the Law Courts, Navy and Army, Aristocracy and Middle Class, the Pre-Raphaelites and the Aesthetes,[16] Imperialism and Feminism, Tennyson and Browning, Flag-waving and Republicanism, the Police and Limited Companies—all these and many lesser subjects served their turn. The cheerful way with which Britons took this lampooning and the joy with which Americans stole it for their own fun suggested that in sense of humor and love of witty words and music, at least, the two peoples were not far apart.

14 Its leading figures were Sidney Olivier, G. B. Shaw, Graham Wallas, and Sidney Webb.

15 W. S. Gilbert, alone a mediocre playwright, although a superb practitioner in the peculiarly English field of nonsense verse; and A. S. Sullivan, alone an undistinguished composer. Both were knighted, but Gilbert had to wait until Edward VII succeeded serious-minded Victoria.

16 In the persons of Algernon Swinburne and Oscar Wilde.

At the end of the century Mr. Dooley of Archey Road, Chicago,[17] observing the conduct of the South African and Spanish-American wars, shrewdly and amusingly drew attention to the fact that Britons and Americans were in much the same box so far as imperialism went, and it was Rudyard Kipling of India, Vermont, and England who sonorously urged the United States to "take up the White Man's burden" in the Philippines. Yet the South African War was the meeting place for so many crosscurrents of purely British development and such a crucial turning-point in domestic and imperial history that its qualities ought not to be lost in a tempting international comparison.

The key figure in these developments was the erstwhile radical, Joseph Chamberlain, who seems to have decided during the Great Depression that, until Britain became much more prosperous, the nation could not afford the program of social welfare which he had once espoused. With foreign competition so severe and foreign markets so difficult to enter, the empire seemed to him to offer the only way out. He split and crippled the Liberal party in 1886 by carrying out of it the Unionists who defeated Gladstone's attempts to give Home Rule to Ireland, and he began to encourage the formation of a group of men who would work for a federation of the self-governing parts of the empire which would serve as the core of a close-knit, tariff-protected, economic union of the whole.

Some of these men were former colonial administrators of an unreflective type; some were hard-headed "development men" who could find the money and the means for exploiting anything profitable, from palm oil to diamonds; and one of them was an executive genius named Cecil

[17] The creation of Finley Peter Dunne.

Rhodes who had translated John Ruskin's misty Oxford lectures into dreams of an ever-expanding empire of self-governing states associated with Great Britain by ties of common culture and free political institutions. His trouble was that since one life was too short, he tried to hurry up the realization of his dreams.

The situation in southern Africa was loaded with explosive contradictions. The original mixed Dutch and Huguenot stock, known as the Boers, formed a pastoral, farming folk whose patriarchal, Old Testament society had regarded the overwhelming native population in a different light from the slave-freeing, missionary-supporting Britons. But, like the American Mormons at a later date, most of them had settled the question by "trekking" from the coastal regions in order to set up two inland republics (Transvaal and Orange Free State) and to avoid exasperating conflicts with British Cape Colony and Natal. Unlike the Mormons, their governments were unassuming and their citizenry loose-footed and resentful of authority. By the 'nineties, thanks to the vigor of Rhodes and the wealth which he drew from Cape Colony's diamond mines at Kimberley, the Boer republics were ringed about by British colonies and protectorates.

The bone of contention proved to be exploitation of the world's greatest gold field near Johannesburg in the Transvaal. Naturally, Britons and Americans, not Boers, had developed these mines, and outside money had financed them. Johannesburg had changed from a Boer market town into something a good deal more like Sacramento or Denver. The Boers resisted the admission of "Uitlanders" to citizenship, taxed them heavily, and showed no interest in spending the money on ordinary urban amenities for "Jo'burg." Both sides were asking for trouble when Rhodes rendered it inevitable by an unsuccessful attempt to stimulate an uprising. Then the German Emperor, Wilhelm II, made matters worse by fishing in these troubled waters. In consequence, Chamberlain was able to carry the British government with him in presenting the Transvaal with what amounted to the choice between submission and war. The Boers chose war in 1899.

It took three humiliating years for the world's greatest empire to defeat two little Boer republics. The brilliant and stubborn guerilla warfare of about eighty thousand Boers changed the course of the British Empire. It ended Britain's lordly foreign policy of "magnificent isolation," for it was a humbling experience to discover how happy most of the rest of the world was made by Britain's incompetence as a bully. The United States and some of the self-governing colonies were the only friends in sight. Britain therefore judged it wise to reinforce American support at once by submitting to some "Big Stick" pressure at the hands of President Theodore Roosevelt and a belligerent Congress. The United Kingdom surrendered her treaty rights in a Panama canal, acknowledged American supremacy in the Caribbean, and allowed political considerations to modify supposedly judicial procedure in the settlement of the Alaska Boundary.

Furthermore, by settling in 1904 imperialistic conflicts with France, which was already in alliance with Russia, and reaching a similar understanding with Russia in 1907, Great Britain completed in a vague way the Triple Entente which confronted the Triple Alliance formed by Germany, Austria, and Italy between 1879 and 1882. In 1902, a regional pact with a rising Japan lightened British responsibilities in the Far East and at that time did not conflict with an almost common Anglo-American front in behalf of the

"Open Door" for various kinds of enterprise in helpless China.

Perhaps equally important was the fashion in which the South African War reinforced Canadian resistance to Chamberlain's policy of imperial centralization and thus, so far as British colonists of European stock were concerned, ensured the achievement of what came to be called "Dominion Status" and ultimately brought about the free and equal association of the dominions with the United Kingdom. By rare and unprecedented wisdom on the parts of Boers and Britons [18] alike, the war was swiftly followed by reconstruction at British expense, by self-government for the two Boer states, and, in 1910, by the establishment of the Union of South Africa, with Louis Botha, the commander of the Boer army in the war, as Prime Minister for both Boer and British constituent states. Australia had become a dominion by the federation of her separate colonies in 1901, and New Zealand had attained the same status in 1907. Further evidence that the old imperialism was dying and that the new conception of empire was to be extended to non-European subjects as well came in 1909, when the Morley-Minto reforms in India began what Morley said was to be a progressive substitution of Indian for British authority there. In 1911, King George and Queen Mary visited India and held a Durbar at Delhi.

Finally, the South African War shook up domestic British politics in a very healthy way. The Conservatives had brought on the war, but once it began, national pride was at stake, and many of the Liberals fell into line. In fact, even the socialist intellectuals of the Fabian Society found a reason for supporting the British cause on the ground that

[18] Most of the British credit is due to the Liberals who supplanted the Conservatives in 1905.

technical advances had made the existence of small nations
no longer defensible. Yet millions of British consciences
were stirred by remorse, particularly in Nonconformist
circles and among Liberals whose ancient orthodoxy prescribed pacifism and proscribed imperialism. Stubborn free-
traders, too, particularly the workers, who were passionately
devoted to the cause of the "free breakfast table," were
suspicious of Chamberlain's intentions, for in order to
create his system of imperial preferential tariffs the United
Kingdom would have to become protectionist.

In his earlier days, Chamberlain had once imprudently
asked: "What ransom will property pay for the security
which it enjoys?" Both parties had by 1902 been paying
that ransom for two generations in the form of installments
of social legislation, but Labor had grown tired of petty
bargaining with them and the Trade Union Congress, having settled its internal problems, had decided in 1900 to
strike out for direct Labor party representation in a systematic way. For one thing, the Home Rule struggle, the South
African War, and an inanition which descended on the
Conservatives under A. J. Balfour, as he tried to dodge
Chamberlain's protectionism, had reduced social reform
to a mere trickle. For another, a recent court decision had
made the future of trade unionism precarious in the extreme and Labor wanted statutory protection.

In 1905, Balfour resigned, and the Liberals under Sir
Henry Campbell-Bannerman formed a new government.
This elderly Scotsman had somehow held together the anti-
Boer and pro-Boer wings of the Liberal party and had
discovered that there was more virtue and strength in the
latter than among the war party of the somewhat shallow,
if decorative, Lord Rosebery who had preceded him as
leader. In 1906, at a general election, the voters confirmed

Campbell-Bannerman's judgment, for they responded enthusiastically to condemnation of recent Conservative policies and rejected Conservative candidates on a wholesale scale. Moreover, they returned twenty-nine members of the new Labor party and about as many Liberals pledged to represent Labor. Counting Labor and the Irish Nationalists on his side, Campbell-Bannerman had over five hundred supporters in the Commons as against about one hundred and fifty.

The new Prime Minister died not long after he had shown his statesmanship by accepting the simple Trades Disputes Bill proposed by the Laborites in place of the complicated piece of legislation produced by the lawyers of his own party, and he was succeeded by H. H. Asquith in 1908. The Liberal government, subsequently sustained in two appeals to the country, now proceeded to carry out the peaceful revolution which transformed Great Britain from modified individualism into a social welfare state. In all this, they owed a good deal to the German social legislation introduced by Bismarck in the 'eighties, and they got some of their information about British conditions from the painstaking researches of the latter-day Benthamites of the Fabian Society, but fundamentally they succeeded in their reforms because they responded to democratic demands instead of trying to elude them. They did not kill socialism by kindness, but they somewhat more than kept up with formulated demands.

We have already noticed the enlightened Liberal South African policy and the acceptance, which accompanied and followed it, of the right of the dominions to retain control of their own policies. The Liberals began their domestic legislation at once by establishing the employer's liability in workmen's compensation and by protecting the rights and activities of trade unions. They followed this up with statutes establishing noncontributory old-age pensions, national labor exchanges, minimum wage boards for the control of "sweatshops," housing and town-planning authorities, and other provisions for public health and child welfare. Their next great objective was a system of unemployment and sickness insurance which should handle in twentieth-century fashion the problems of what the Elizabethan Poor Laws had called "the able-bodied poor" and "the poor not able to work."

At this point the House of Lords decided to call a halt to the advance towards socialism. Ever since the Glorious Revolution, this predominantly conservative, unrepresentative body had been prudent about thwarting the representative House, but following the transition to democracy, Conservative minorities in the Commons had from time to time encouraged it to exercise its veto against Liberal bills. Balfour, in particular, had played this dangerous game much too often. Now he had, in an astute Welsh Chancellor of the Exchequer, David Lloyd George, an opponent who boldly answered this defiance of democracy by carrying in the Commons a budget whose offensive land and other taxation was a clear invitation, which the Lords accepted, to break established precedent by rejecting a money bill. The ensuing violent struggle, marked by two bitterly contested elections which made the Liberals dependent on Irish and Labor support, ended with the completion of British political democracy. This was accomplished by the Parliament Act of 1911, by which the veto power of the Lords became merely suspensive, money bills were removed from their control, and the duration of Parliaments was limited to five years. By another act of 1911, Members of Parliament at last received salaries, thus easing the position of Labor Members and fulfilling the last but one of the Chartist demands.[19]

The projected social insurance was then enacted. In addition, a series of widespread strikes brought about the statutory establishment of minimum wages for miners in 1912. Finally, Ireland received her reward for support of the Liberals in the form of a Home Rule Act which became law in 1914 after it had been three times turned down by the House of Lords. It is a measure of the ineradicable emotions and prejudices involved in the ancient Anglo-Irish tragedy (for the economic issues had been reduced to negligible proportions), that the imminent accomplishment of this surrender to Irish nationalism provoked preparations for armed resistance in Protestant Ulster and mutiny among the British army officers in Ireland just before the act was suspended for the duration of the war which broke out in 1914.[20]

That war had been brewing ever since the headstrong German Kaiser, Wilhelm II, had cut free from canny old Prince Bismarck in 1890 and had allowed Russo-German understanding to collapse. Russia and France had promptly formed a defensive alliance against Germany, Austria, and Italy, and Great Britain had loosely aligned herself with France and Russia in 1904 and 1907. The issues at stake between the two camps were not primarily contests for overseas resources and markets, since colonies and "spheres of influence" in Africa, Asia, and the Pacific islands had been neatly divided up among the powers by a series of agreements between 1880 and 1907 and were to continue to be. The real contest was for acknowledged leadership in

[19] The unsatisfied demand was for annually chosen parliaments.

[20] The Liberal Cabinet had had to pay its debts to the Irish and Labor Members, but it was able to defer surrender to the vigorous, and often violent, campaign for woman suffrage.

Europe, and the region which invited rivalry was the decaying Turkish Empire and the land bridge of the Balkans between it and Europe. This meant that friction was greatest, and most likely to cause trouble, between the two rashest European powers, Austria and Russia; but their chief backers, Germany and France, could not escape being involved in any serious test of strength.

Great Britain retained great freedom of action, for it was to her interest to preserve peace in the world and, on the whole, Britons felt that the best way to do that was to try to maintain a balance of power on the Continent. From 1898 onwards, that is, both before and after the colonial settlements with France and Russia, Britain made repeated attempts to reach an understanding with Germany, but the Germans felt too strong to have to subordinate their ambitions in any way to the operations of the exasperating British balance wheel. They saw clearly that Britain's real strength was naval, and they began in 1898 to build ships on an unparalleled scale as a counterpoise to the weight which Britain could throw to the side of France and Russia. This was a challenge which even pacifistic Liberals dared not ignore; and it is evidence of the "prosperity" which was felt in Great Britain from 1896 to about 1913, that the nation managed to carry enormous naval expenditures as well as the costs of the new social legislation. Great Britain, dependent on imported foodstuffs, was good for less than six months in any war in which she did not possess naval superiority.

It is unnecessary to detail the preliminary trials of prestige strength which converted Europe into an armed camp by 1914, but it is well to remember that behind Germany's confidence lay the unmistakable fact that on the economic front she was beating Great Britain at her own game. She had passed Britain by a large margin in sales to Continental markets, she was cutting into the British lead in markets overseas, and by generous subsidies to shipping lines she was skimming off the cream of the world carrying trade which had been a British preserve since about 1860.

In brief, Germany believed that her disciplined efforts and her intelligent organization had made her the strongest single instrument of co-ordinated power in the world and that she ought to be recognized as such. She was not afraid of Russia and France and she believed that if war came Britons could not resist the choice open to them of keeping out and reaping the profits of neutrality.

Great Britain's chief fault in this whole matter was that her governments did not declare unmistakably that they would assist France and Russia, although no outright alliances with them existed.[21] The answer to that, while it contributed nothing towards clarifying the situation, was that no government, Liberal or Conservative, could have made such declarations and remained in power, for the British democracy was almost as resolutely opposed to "entangling alliances" as the American. And time seems to have shown that, even if the declarations might have been made, they could only have postponed the conflict. Human intelligence has not yet proved capable of finding a solution for "the German Problem." Mankind has not yet agreed upon the machinery and procedure by which the international community can peacefully accommodate itself to great alterations in the uneasy balance of national powers and ambitions.

When the war came on August 1, 1914, arising out of Austro-Russian conflict in the Balkans, the British Cabinet

[21] British and French military and naval staffs had framed plans for joint action if war came.

was about equally divided. Sir Edward Grey tried to keep the war from spreading beyond Russia and Austria, but he did not either assure France of support, or tell Germany that France would get it, until the Conservatives had made it plain that they insisted on standing by France and Russia in the war which had begun. Grey then promised to use the British fleet to protect French coasts and shipping against Germany. The German ultimatum to, and invasion of, neutralized Belgium completed the work, for protection of the Low Countries from powerful dominance was the oldest principle of British foreign policy—to say nothing of Britain's guarantee of Belgian neutrality. When Germany ignored a British counterultimatum, Great Britain entered the war at midnight, August 4th. Two members of the Cabinet, John Burns and John Morley, resigned rather than agree.

It was, of course, a world war, and for six months or so the British military effort, although of superb quality, was small. After a brief war of movement in which Germany failed to knock out France and Russia in quick succession, the main land warfare settled down to lines of trenches from the North Sea to the Alps, from the Alps to the Adriatic, and from the Baltic to the Black Sea and Mediterranean. The use of aircraft, poison gas, and tanks could not seriously alter its character. There were other fronts in Egypt and the Near East, at the Dardanelles, in Macedonia, in Mesopotamia, in East Africa, and at other points where Germans overseas bowed to isolation and superior force. Italy deserted to the Entente, Turkey sided with the Central Powers, and Japan not only fulfilled her obligations to Great Britain in the Pacific but seized the opportunity to prey upon China. The British dominions and colonies rallied to the Allied cause in an impressive and effective way.

The Turks and Germans foiled an attempt to open up a supply route for Russia through the Bosphorus and the Black Sea, thus condemning what was economically the most backward member of the Entente to rely almost exclusively on her own resources.

On land, the Central Powers distinctly more than held their own against the Entente, but they could not force a decision, and meanwhile the British navy was enforcing a blockade which threatened to ensure victory to the Entente. The German navy attempted once, in May, 1916, to shatter the blockade, but Admiral Jellicoe, who alone "could have lost the war in an afternoon," maintained British control of the seas at the price of a naval battle off Jutland which involved over two hundred and fifty vessels and in which his forces lost more heavily than the Germans. In these circumstances, Germany turned to a counterblockade through the ruthless submarine warfare against merchant and passenger shipping which she had relaxed in the face of general and, in particular, of American disapproval shortly after the wholesale destruction of civilians in the sinking of the *Lusitania* early in 1915.

By 1917 Italy, Russia, and France were weakening on land, and unrestricted submarine warfare was progressively exhausting Great Britain. Credit for supplies from the United States was almost at an end. But in April, 1917, the United States entered the war, and in spite of an Italian collapse, Russian revolution and withdrawal, and mutiny in the French army, British resolution continued to hold firm. British and dominion forces, now numbering millions,[22] not only took on added responsibilities, but won substantial successes at very high cost on the Western Front

[22] About six million were mobilized from the British Isles and about three million from the Empire.

in their effort to maintain the balance when German armies came west from Russia while France was reorganizing her army.

American financial and industrial support was made available at once, the American navy co-operated quickly with the British in the exacting new methods which curbed submarine warfare in the summer of 1917, and huge, fresh American armies were made available in France by the summer of 1918 just after the Germans had in vain made three last amazing efforts to break through the Western Front before American numbers could be brought to bear. The tide turned in the middle of July, and the whole great structure of the Central Powers, from Mesopotamia, through Palestine, the Balkans, and Italy, to France and Belgium, was smashed by continuous and irresistible Allied assaults. The German fleet refused to leave harbor to attack the British, the Kaiser abdicated, and a provisional German government agreed on November 11, 1918, to an armistice on the basis of President Wilson's "Fourteen Points."

CHAPTER X

Defense of Democratic Welfare
1919–1939

BETWEEN JANUARY 12th and May 7th, 1919, the victors composed the principal peace treaty in Paris without consulting the vanquished. Of the men who decided on its main outlines—Georges Clemenceau, David Lloyd George, and Woodrow Wilson—only the American aimed almost consistently at fundamental improvement of the international community. Yet his own people had turned against his plans two months before the negotiations began, whereas the Frenchman and the Briton maintained popular support. Wilson, too assured in his idealism, failed to compromise with human nature. Clemenceau and George played too much upon hysterical demands for security and revenge. The treaty's beneficial qualities were therefore considerably offset by reactionary financial and territorial exactions. French security was separately underwritten by a proposed Anglo-American guarantee which ran counter to the traditional foreign policies of both countries and which collapsed when the United States Senate refused to ratify it, thus intensifying French determination to find other assurances.

Wilson's Fourteen Points could be reduced to the right of self-determination for national entities, varying in de-

gree according to their capacity for self-government; freedom to navigate the seas in peace and war; the removal of
international economic barriers and the reduction of armaments; and "a general association of nations" (the League
of Nations) designed to secure "mutual guarantees of political independence and territorial integrity to great and
small states alike." [1] Before the Armistice had been concluded, Wilson, at the insistence of Great Britain and
France, had had to drop "freedom of the seas" and had had
to add compensation for damage done to the civilian population and their property "by land, by sea, and from the air."
These and later surrenders, chiefly by way of a number of
permanent or temporary violations of self-determination in
drawing new national boundaries in Europe and Asia, were
reflected in provisions of the treaty, but they rightly seemed
to Wilson of less importance than his success in making
the League of Nations an integral part of it. The Germans
signed the treaty on June 28, 1919, after ineffectual protests
against its departures from the Fourteen Points and the
Armistice understandings. They scuttled their fleet after its
surrender to Great Britain at Scapa Flow.

In the United States, a ruthless anti-Wilson alliance defeated all of the President's policies [2] and rapidly set about
segregating the country by means of tariffs and immigration
restrictions. A brief but severe depression accelerated efforts to collect some of the enormous sums lent to the Allies.
That meant that Great Britain and France, and to a lesser
degree Italy, Japan, and the secondary powers, had to try
to enforce the treaty and to set up the League of Nations

[1] Wilson was neither the inventor nor the architect of the League, but
was its most devoted supporter.

[2] The treaty (and the League), the guarantee to France, responsibilities
as a mandatory in former Turkey, and participation in determining the
amount of German reparations.

and at the same time make terms with the aloof United States. From the beginning, these efforts were fatally hamstrung by three circumstances. Germany and Russia were not members of the League. Great Britain aimed at the rehabilitation of Germany for the sake of the general economic revival which she needed for her recovery, while France insisted on keeping Germany weak and setting up against her such heavily armed satellites that she could not become a menace again. Finally, the principal instrument at the League's disposal for the enforcement of its will against aggressors was economic blockade, in other words, the British navy, whereas the chief potential objector to such "sanctions" was the United States, with which Great Britain was determined to keep friendly. In these circumstances, it is remarkable that the international situation did not deteriorate more rapidly than it did.

With Germany's navy and merchant marine gone, much of her former coal, iron, and industry under foreign control, and her colonial empire divided up among the victors under the League's system of mandates, Britain could begin to reduce her own commitments. She had been the financial backer of the Entente as long as her resources lasted and after that the borrower from the United States in their behalf. Her debtors could not or, as in the case of Russia, would not pay, and the United States rejected the suggestion of writing off an amount of the British debt equal to the amount which Britain would forgive her debtors. The resultant burden on the British taxpayer was so enormous that he revolted against continued expenditures on overseas adventures, as for instance against Bolshevist Russia, or to maintain British authority in Mesopotamia, Egypt, and Ireland. Labor, especially, was sympathetic with the

Russian Revolution and with nationalistic aspirations within the empire. Wilson's espousal of "self-determination" for national entities was a mighty force in the world from 1918 onwards.

During the war, the dominions had been directly represented on the central British executive authority, the Imperial War Cabinet, and this principle had been continued at the peace conference and in the League of Nations. Canada even held up the final royal signature of the treaty until it had been ratified by her Parliament.

Also during the war, the Irish nationalists had once more seen their chance in British preoccupation elsewhere and had rebelled unsuccessfully in 1916. The rebellion had had little popular support, but the martyrdoms which attended its repression converted Sinn Fein, the revolutionary party, into the cause of Irish freedom, and Sinn Fein courageously and ingeniously organized the severance of Ireland from Britain. The Irish moderates were helpless while savage guerilla war raged between the revolutionaries and the British forces. The immediate outcome was that in 1921 southern Ireland became a dominion. Further bitter and sometimes sanguinary struggles had to be fought, both within the Irish Free State and against the terms of the 1921 treaty, before the quasi-republic of Eire established domestic order and cut itself almost entirely free from the British Commonwealth.[3]

Irish nationalism was an old problem, but newer nationalisms were no less vigorous and Britain bowed to them. In 1922, Egypt, which had been made a protectorate in 1915, was declared an independent country, with reservations as

[3] New constitution, 1937, and new settlement of all outstanding Anglo-Irish issues except the partition of the island, 1938.

to defense of Suez, special rights for foreigners, and responsibility for the Sudan.[4] In 1921, a constitutional monarchy was set up in the mandate of Iraq (Mesopotamia), which entered the League as an independent state in 1932. The Arab-Jewish problem bedeviled Palestine, another Class A mandate, so profoundly and bloodily that the two nationalisms canceled each other so far as progress towards independence was concerned. In fact, a British commission in 1937 recommended division of the small country into separate Arabic and Jewish states, but this pleased neither party and no settlement was reached.

It was India which posed the problem of nationalism within the empire most severely, and here there began in 1919 a stubborn war of attrition against British sovereignty which recalled Ireland's efforts during the previous century. The deep complexities of the situation in British India and the Native States, with their many peoples, languages, religions, and castes, could be mildly paralleled only in Soviet Russia or in China. The most imposing nationalisms were those of the Hindu community and of the more powerful of the Native States, but the Moslem community was large and warlike, and the "submerged classes" of the caste system were so numerous that they could not be ignored. In the circumstances, Britain adopted compromise policies. British India, in both the provincial and the central governments, was to be given more and more self-government over a period during which British civil servants could be replaced by Indians.

The principle of dyarchy suggested by Lord Durham for Canada in 1839 (and applied by the United States to the

---

[4] An alliance as of equals was concluded in 1936, with joint rule of the Sudan. Egypt entered the League in 1937.

Philippines a century later), by which departments of government were handed over to complete Indian control, began in the provincial governments in 1919. Next year Mohandas Gandhi started his ingenious efforts to broaden these concessions into complete home rule, and (in spite of the fact that Gandhi advocated a return to handicrafts) his party, the Indian Nationalist Congress, received increasing support from the growing large-scale Indian industries. There was inevitably a great deal of violence on both sides —chiefly British, but also Indian, in spite of Gandhi's advocacy of nonviolence. A further substantial surrender to self-government in 1935 ended dyarchy in the provinces, leaving Great Britain in control of the central government until the Princes of the Native States should federate with it. Even after that federation should have taken place, however, the governor-general was to retain control of defense, foreign relations, and religion.

Few observers doubted that dominion status and independence would somehow follow, but there were misgivings about the applicability of western parliamentary institutions to Indian circumstances, particularly when it appeared that the Congress party, overwhelmingly Hindu, was thinking in terms of one-party rule along lines analogous to those of China, Japan, and Russia. Britain was less concerned economically by this time because her stake in the Indian Civil Service had become quite small and because, when the gold standard for the pound ended in 1931, India began a continuous process of repatriating British investments on a colossal scale. But, as in the case of Ireland, pride, prestige, and tradition could not lightly be disregarded, and strategic advantages could not be given up without a struggle. India seemed to be fated to follow the same bitter road towards freedom as southern Ireland, and to pay a much larger price in internal suffering before tolerable unity could be obtained.

For the older dominions there was no struggle of any great importance. The war efforts of Australia, Canada, New Zealand, and South Africa had converted them into nations on their own. New Zealand was, for various reasons, more British than Britain herself, and Australia tended to accept the British lead. But in the League and elsewhere South Africa and the Irish Free State were determined to make the world recognize their separate status, and Canada was not far behind.

In fact, the North American dominion, through a combination of circumstances, chief of which was her inescapable role of completing an economic and political triangle with Great Britain and the United States, single-handed changed the course of British Far Eastern policy at an Imperial Conference in 1921. Her Prime Minister persuaded that group of Prime Ministers and Cabinet members, already committed to renewal of the Anglo-Japanese Alliance, to shelve it in favor of negotiations for a multilateral Pacific Agreement. The Washington Conference of 1921–22, which was promptly built upon this opportunity by the American Secretary of State, C. E. Hughes, completed the work by treaties for scrapping a large number of naval vessels; for establishing a ratio of 5–5–3–1.75–1.75 for the capital ships of Great Britain, the United States, Japan, France, and Italy; for the withdrawal of Japan from her adventures in China; and for the agreement to respect the existing Pacific situation [5] and to refer future disputes to joint conference.

---

[5] Particularly "the sovereignty, the independence, and the territorial and administrative integrity of China."

In the light of these circumstances, law was belatedly catching up with reality when the Imperial Conference of 1926 and the Statute of Westminster of 1931 finally got round to formulating the relationship existing among Great Britain, Canada, Australia, New Zealand, South Africa, Newfoundland [6] and the Irish Free State. The statute crystallized as best it could the pronouncement (probably phrased by Balfour) of 1926:

> They are autonomous communities within the British Empire, equal in status, in no way subordinate one to another in any aspect of their domestic or external affairs, though united by a common allegiance to the crown, and freely associated as members of the British Commonwealth of Nations.

In other words, none of the group could act so as to bind any other except by previous agreement.

While all this had been going on abroad, Britons had had plenty of problems to wrestle with at home. Just as in 1815, so in 1919, there were debt, inflation, and unemployment to be faced, but the political forces had radically altered. Agriculture and the land were no longer influential; industry wanted protection instead of free trade; and finance yearned for the gold standard and easy movement of goods in order to compete with New York and Paris. But now the people had votes and they intended to use them in order to protect the standard of money wages and the much-extended social legislation which they had achieved since 1906, and to preserve the free importation of commodities which made their money go farther. All in all, therefore, the two principal propertied classes were at odds between themselves and, in their anxiety to reduce taxation and production costs, both were at odds with Labor.

In 1815, Britain had had a running head start in the

[6] Bankruptcy was to terminate this rather unreal status in 1933.

international race for wealth from industrialization. In 1919, other countries had caught up with and even passed her in some ways, because of superior natural resources and inventive skill, cheaper labor, and less handicap from obsolete equipment. This was true not merely of the United States, Germany, France, and Belgium, but of newcomers as well. Japan had made such enormous strides in industry, particularly in the field of cotton textiles which had once been Britain's own, and in combining this with unified finance, selling organizations, and mercantile marine, that she was no longer a market, but a deadly competitor in markets everywhere. Large-scale industry and protective tariffs were soon to transform India and China in somewhat the same way, although to a lesser extent. In protectionist Canada industrial production now exceeded agricultural. The Russian market was closed, the American market was narrowing rapidly, and the German and other Continental markets were prostrate.

France and Italy did not need British coal because they were getting German coal by way of war reparations. Oil products were replacing coal as fuel for many forms of power. The electric dynamo and its transmission systems not only delivered power more conveniently than steam, but produced larger amounts from the same amount of coal, when it was used.[7] All in all, international trade was contracting and Britain's share in it was growing smaller, thus throwing her weakened basic industries still farther out of joint, starving her merchant marine, and almost shutting down the shipbuilding industry.

Other countries eased similar situations at the expense

[7] Comparing 1936 with 1920, five times as much electrical power was produced by twice as much coal.

of investors by devaluing their currencies, but "the City,"
that is, the British financial community, was determined
to restore the pound sterling to its old gold value, partly
for the sake of sustaining British investments at home and
overseas, but largely in order to restore London to its profitable position as banker and insurer for the outside world.
The City rightly believed that Paris would have its troubles
with the devalued franc and that New York lacked the
accumulated skill and organization necessary to reap full
advantages from the transformation of the United States
from a debtor to a creditor country. In this policy the City
had Labor as a half-conscious ally, not because their ultimate aims were similar, but because Labor did not want
any lowering in the value of existing money wages and
social insurance benefits.

What Britain had to do after 1918 was to change over
her economy, thus adding endless dislocations and com-
plications to the distorted postwar situation. The country
vigorously set out to do this in dozens of ways, at the same
time balancing the budget by unparalleled peacetime taxation, and supporting millions of temporarily or permanently
unemployed persons, either through extension of the social
insurance structure or by poor relief out of local taxation.[8]

This remarkable transformation was overlooked by most
observers, for taxation, unemployment, and unrest were
much easier to see. Yet between 1923 and 1938 the contrac-
tion in the employment afforded by old industrial dependa-
bles like coal, woolens, cotton, iron, and steel was a good
deal more than compensated for by the expansion of the
electrical and the internal-combustion motor industries,

[8] Probably the average of unemployment, 1850–1914, was 4½ per cent.
For 1921–37 it was over 14 per cent.

building, various light industries, and widespread increases in the service groups.[9]

An economy which had been geared for exports was changed into one which catered for the home market. Whereas in 1911 exports of British products were equivalent to 22 per cent of the national income and retained imports were equivalent to 28 per cent, in 1935 the corresponding figures for a money income twice as large were 10.8 and 17.7 per cent. Naturally these developments slowed down, and occasionally reversed, the nation's accumulation of capital wealth.

In most parts of the world, including Great Britain, governments intervened increasingly during the period between the wars in economic affairs, sometimes to favor producers, sometimes to protect the consumers or labor, and sometimes to promote the "national interest." These practices were undertaken partly to meet international competition, partly to meet the demands of universal suffrage,[10] but most of all to counter the growth and the power of amalgamations and monopolies. The responses of British economic groups to this intervention varied considerably. For instance, the British railways were consolidated, with governmental encouragement, into four regional monopolies under close public rate regulation. The declining coal, iron, and cotton industries successfully resisted governmental control. Agriculture, after suffering profound shocks during the early 'twenties, gratefully became the special care of government, whose marketing boards, subsidies, and milk distribution schemes came into play just when

[9] Employment of insured persons, aged sixteen to sixty-four, increased on balance by 21.5 per cent. Note that this was in spite of great increases in labor-saving devices.

[10] British women received the vote in two installments, in 1918 and 1928.

mechanization and scientific research were ready to promote an agricultural revolution in Great Britain.

Coal presented a special problem because unemployed miners were not easily employable in other pursuits, and because the mines were frequently located in semirural districts which were unable to support out of local taxes large numbers of unemployed who had exhausted their insurance benefits. Many uneconomic pits were shut down and employment at the better mines was irregular. There was a national miners' strike in 1920, but matters really came to a head in 1925 when the coalowners announced that the miners' cherished seven-hour day must be lengthened and wages cut. The Conservative Prime Minister, Stanley Baldwin, postponed the issue by a temporary governmental subsidy, but he refused to continue this in 1926 when an investigatory commission reported, in effect, that either a great many unprofitable mines must shut down or hours must be lengthened and wages reduced.

This was the occasion for a new kind of trial of strength by organized Labor, which had recently been amalgamating its unions and had set up a General Council of the Trade Union Congress to create a united front in industrial disputes. The council called for sympathetic strikes to aid the miners and received well-disciplined support from the railwaymen, iron and steel workers, the builders' unions, and the printing trades. The government refused to make any concessions to this alliance and received broad support from the middle class in maintaining essential services, because this "General Strike" threatened fundamental change in the established order of things. In these circumstances, the inexperienced council did not know what to do and could only advise the men to go back to work, which they did. The miners hung on grimly, however, until Neville

Chamberlain systematically starved them into submission.[11] Next year, Parliament passed a statute which declared sympathetic strikes illegal and considerably limited trade-union activities.

Two years later, the Labor party, for the second time since 1918,[12] was entrusted with the formation of a national government and was thus fated to grapple with the world depression which began with the American stock-market crash of October, 1929. As before, it did not have an over-all majority, for although the Liberal party had become increasingly negligible since the Lloyd George Coalition of 1916 and was the minority party in the Commons, it still returned enough members to hold the balance of power between the Conservatives and Labor unless the voters gave the former a clear majority. In critical times, the British voter backed the Conservatives, but when things were going well, as in the summer of 1929, he was prepared to let Labor attempt reforms. Now J. R. MacDonald and his colleagues had about 285 seats and the Conservatives about 260, so that the Liberals' 60 odd were a brake on the government.

MacDonald and his party made relatively little mark on the internal development of Britain, since he himself was more distinguished for worthy intentions and persuasive rhetoric than for practical plans, Philip Snowden was as orthodox a Chancellor of the Exchequer as Gladstone, and Sidney Webb (Lord Passfield) was a well-known gradualist and researcher. As over against these "intellectuals," the two outstanding former workers in the Cabinet, "Uncle Arthur" Henderson and J. H. Thomas, did not really pre-

[11] As Minister of Health, by forbidding local authorities to use public funds for relief.

[12] The first was an unexpected term of nine months in 1924 under J. R. MacDonald.

sume to lead. The grave, indeed almost the single, problem of 1929 to 1931 was unemployment, and the Labor party gradually split wide open as it became clear that Snowden would insist on balancing the budget even if it meant reduction in the state's social services.

Suddenly, in the summer of 1931, after almost two years of deepening world depression, the dams which Britons had been building against economic deluge broke. The City, which "borrowed short and lent long," that is, acted as the world's banker, faced a panicky run on the bank by foreign depositors which it could not meet with specie payments. New York and Paris, concerned though they were to maintain London's stability, would not help without assurances of far-reaching economies, and these, Snowden said, could be made only in the social services.

The divided Labor Cabinet thereupon resigned, but MacDonald arranged with the King to form a so-called National government to balance the budget and save the pound sterling. Actually, of course, it was a Conservative government for which MacDonald, Snowden, and a few other Laborites and Liberals formed a thin façade. In spite of its formation, the gold standard was abandoned within less than a month. The National government promptly went to the country in a confused, hysterical election which it won overwhelmingly, so that it faced only a tiny opposition composed chiefly of fifty-two Laborites and four stubborn Liberal members of Lloyd George's family.

This government, like the American government almost two years later, benefited immensely by the elasticity which returned to economic life when the rigid bonds of the gold standard were broken. The pound did not decline in domestic purchasing power because world prices were falling and foreign suppliers of raw materials wanted to sell at

any price. But industry, having triumphed at last over the
City's financial orthodoxy and, in the form of cuts in public
salaries and social services, over Labor's own chosen citadel,
was now determined that Britain should not be a dumping
ground for the rest of the world. Without a precise mandate
on the subject, Baldwin's Conservatives set about introducing systematic, if low, tariff protection.[13]

In 1932, the future of trade among the English-speaking
countries of the world hung in the balance. Normally, the
largest triangular exchange of goods, services, and investment in the world was that embracing Great Britain, the
United States, and Canada.[14] In 1930, the United States
under the Smoot-Hawley Act had set its tariffs prohibitively
high and Canada had reciprocated because she had to keep
her citizens from buying American goods lest she be unable to get together enough American dollars to pay interest on her borrowings in the United States. She had also
appealed unsuccessfully to the British Labor government
to adopt protection, so that imperial preferences could be
granted and a great closed imperial economy could be set
up. The National government [15] agreed to discuss this pro-
posal in an imperial conference at Ottawa in the summer
of 1932. The American Congress, by setting tariffs still
higher about a month before the meeting took place, almost
defiantly invited the Ottawa conferees to do their worst.

[13] They also reduced their war-debt payments to the United States
to annual "tokens," practically canceled German reparations and Allied
war debts to Britain, and unsuccessfully urged international agreement on
disarmament and on the drastic reduction of the tariff and administrative
barriers to world trade which had soared to prohibitive heights.

[14] The trade of the United States with each of the other two was about
equal.

[15] Baldwin was its dominant member, although he did not formally become Prime Minister until 1935.

At Ottawa, in order to preserve some economic unity in a panicky empire, the British government substantially modified its own low tariff policies in response to dominion demands for high protection. This inevitably meant the discouragement of trade with countries outside the Ottawa system and it also meant a large increase in the burden of invisible taxation to be borne by the poorer consumers in Great Britain, the dominions, and some other parts of the empire. But such was the temper created by three years of world depression, and politicians bowed to it. Not until 1935, in the case of Canada, and 1938, in the case of Great Britain, was the United States able through Cordell Hull's prosecution of reciprocal trade treaties to get at least part way inside the Ottawa system.

Attempts have been made [16] to translate the economic developments of the twenty-five years after 1914 into terms which would indicate the changes in the well-being of the masses in Great Britain. In the first place, to quote Beveridge, unemployment relief had shifted "from insurance by contract to relief by status," and it had been supplemented for nearly all workers by a remarkably comprehensive system of other social services at low money levels. Real wages,[17] which were a little below the standard of 1914 in 1924, had risen by about 30 per cent in 1937. The working week was reduced by about 6 hours for most workers during the bitter labor struggles immediately after 1918 to 47 or 48 hours, and, except for 1926 to 1930, the miners had a 7 or 7½ hour day. In all forms of taxation, the working classes carried about 34 per cent of the total in 1914 and

[16] Notably by Sir William Beveridge, A. L. Bowley, Colin Clark, and Lord Stamp.

[17] That is, money wages in terms of the cost of living.

about 28 per cent in 1926, but had their share increased again to about 33 per cent by the adoption of protection after 1931.

During the generation between the South African War and 1933, Britons had shown that it was possible for an empire to slow down its expansion, even to contract at important points, without ceasing to provide a tolerably satisfying life for its peoples.[18] During the same period, universal suffrage and welfare democracy had substantially corrected the traditional bias of government towards favoring the propertied classes. A great war and a great depression had been weathered without the establishment of authoritarian methods at home or marked aggressiveness abroad. Britain had even been able, following France's failure to achieve her ends against Germany by occupation of the Ruhr valley in 1923, to make her view prevail that reparations must be scaled down, and loans be made, in order to rehabilitate Germany and to encourage her to be a co-operative member of the European community and of the League of Nations. Apparently these achievements owed something to accumulated wealth, a great deal to three centuries of practice in compromising opposed views, and perhaps most of all to honest, loyal, and vigorous acceptance of political democracy, for France and the United States revealed quite similar capacities.

The behavior of Japan, Germany, and Italy, as the world depression deepened, international trade dried up, and foreign loans ceased to be available, was directly opposite. Each of these countries submitted to authoritarianism at home and expansionism abroad as a possible way out of the arrested or retrogressive condition in which they found them-

[18] It is a striking fact that migration within the empire was reversed about 1930 and began consistently to flow inwards to Great Britain.

selves. In Japan, a military group, having failed on several occasions to get support by constitutional means or by terrorism, captured the government by force, set up a dictatorship, and embarked on the conquest of Manchuria in defiance of treaty and League obligations. In Germany, the National Socialist German Workers' Party (Nazis), a minority, seized the fatally swollen executive authority of the President, and tried, at first vainly, to absorb Austria. In Italy, a flashy dictator, who had seized power in 1922, ruthlessly concentrated authority in his immediate circle of accomplices and set out to capitalize against France and Britain the "nuisance value" of his essentially weak country's geographical position in the Mediterranean.

These countries, relative to Great Britain, France, and the United States, were poor, and inexperienced in the tolerant political compromise of domestic differences. While political democracy had taken root in all of them, it had proved to be a sickly plant. Germany provided the most illuminating example. Her people had accepted semiabsolutism while the Prussian and imperial regimes had been making a success out of expansionism between 1862 and 1914. They set up a democratic republic in 1918 when they were beaten, humiliated, and stripped of many of their possessions, and that republic responded eagerly to outside aid and encouragement after 1923. Yet, although the German workers believed in democracy, the officer class, the civil service, the judiciary, the great landowners, and industry (organized into monopolies which made American combines look tame) never did.

Consequently, when over three years of depression had produced widespread unemployment, and when foreign assistance dried up, the authoritarian groups defied the republic, reduced it to impotence by fostering cleavages, and, through Germany's much-inflated and senile figurehead, President Hindenburg, in 1933 handed the state over to the Nazi leader, Adolf Hitler, for a resumption of the imperialistic expansion which had worked to their advantage before 1914. That brilliant demagogue had made the achievement easier by convincing a large proportion of the masses that he aimed only at their betterment.

Clearly, the only answer to the Japanese, German, and Italian challenges which would have had any chance of peaceful, or moderately peaceful, success would have been a resolute, united insistence by the other nations of the world that any alteration in the territorial sovereignties of the world or controls of its markets and raw materials must be effected by negotiation under the auspices of the world community as a whole. Many of the smaller states had tried to organize this united front through the League of Nations, but they were defeated by the actions of the bigger states. There were many reasons for this, such as the absence of the United States and Russia from the League, the defiant resignations from it of Germany, Japan, and Italy, or the essential cross-purposes of French and British policies, but at bottom the trouble was that the big nations regarded the League as an instrument to forward their individual policies instead of accepting the limitations on their own freedom of action which its organization into a world authority would have required.

It was no accident that the respectable amount of collective security which existed in 1929 began to evaporate when both Britain and France turned increasingly to bilateral agreements with other nations. It was in February, 1938, that Neville Chamberlain told the House of Commons of his quest for "any common ground on which we might build up a general scheme of appeasement in Europe," but that policy already had a seven-year record of failure because British and other governments had again and again betrayed and blunted the only existing machinery for peaceful change. Things might have been better if American opinion had not refused to support the unmistakable desire of both Republican and Democratic administrations to co-operate with the League after 1931, or if Great Britain could have worked to establish some solid understanding with Russia instead of surrendering to the fear that communism might spread westward across Europe and upset the existing British pattern of life.

As it was, the three aggressors very skillfully isolated their victims and separated their potential opponents. They were like gangsters who assaulted the weak and made separate bargains for increasing amounts of "protection money" from the strong.[19] They were increasingly willing to use outright force, because it became more and more apparent that other governments and the peoples which they represented were willing to pay very high prices, particularly at others' expense, in order to avoid war. Great Britain, France, and the United States, and Russia to a slighter degree, kept hoping that at some time the gangsters would pause to digest their spoils. The governments of Britain and France, being chiefly concerned about Hitler's Germany, came to hope that its expansion towards the east would end up in the exhausting business of grappling with Russia.

The record of aggression was an astonishingly long one: Manchuria in 1931, followed by North China; a failure in Austria in 1934; Abyssinia in 1935; the Rhineland and Spain in 1936; China proper in 1937; Austria and western

[19] The public evidence of this alliance was the Anti-Comintern Pact of November 25, 1936, between Germany and Japan, to which Italy subscribed on November 6, 1937.

Czechoslovakia in 1938; the rest of Czechoslovakia, Albania, Danzig, and Poland in 1939. Parallel to this record of successful aggression there was a record of failure in collective action: treaties flagrantly broken without effective response from the victims, alone or in unison; disarmament conferences which had a way of accelerating rearmament; economic conferences which left things in a worse state than before; League sanctions too timid to achieve their purpose; and such a transparent farce as the "International Committee for the Application of the Agreement Regarding Non-intervention in Spain."

Italy's defiant conquest of Abyssinia in the winter of 1935–36 probably marked the beginning of Britain's effort to regain the ground lost during seventeen years of reduction of armaments.[20] Apparently the Admiralty, or the Cabinet, or both, must have felt remarkably unprepared for war to let Italy treat the Mediterranean, the Suez Canal, and the Red Sea as Italian conveniences. But the road back to armed strength was a long one, and the unawakened British people had just voted overwhelmingly in favor of peaceful change.[21] Trusting to French military prowess and to the Maginot line of fortifications facing Germany, Britain concentrated for the most part on her own navy and air force, but she also brought her small army up to a high degree of efficiency and made military life more attractive by higher pay, some democratization of the officer group, and other innovations.

[20] Japan's denunciation in December, 1934, of the 5-5-3 naval ratio also had some effect, although there was an obvious inclination to treat this as the problem of the United States. But in 1935, the United States began to legislate itself into neutrality.

[21] In the unofficial "Peace Ballots" of early 1935. Of 11½ million who voted, over 11 million depended on the League, 10½ million favored all-round disarmament, 10 million favored economic sanctions, 9½ million wanted abolition of military aircraft, and almost 7 million favored military sanctions.

The government did not dare to introduce the unprecedented policy of peacetime conscription until shortly after Hitler's conquest of Austria in March, 1938.

It must remain an open question, until the evidence becomes public, whether Great Britain failed to call a halt to Hitler's expansion in 1938 because she and France did not feel capable of stopping him, or because they hoped that he would leave them alone while he went on eastwards to an inevitable conflict with Russia. Probably it was for both reasons. At any rate, the calculated humiliation to which Daladier and Neville Chamberlain were subjected at Munich in September, when Hitler made them force Czechoslovakia to surrender, and the reproaches which they received from the rest of the world for their betrayal of the Czechs,[22] made it apparent that no matter how deep the relief that war had been avoided, the British people would now insist on a determined attempt to retrieve the national honor.

At this point, Hitler quite understandingly overreached himself. After the most precise assurances that he would be content with the partial maiming of Czechoslovakia, he proceeded to ignore his engagements, a process which he confidently completed by entering Prague, the national capital, and taking over the whole country in mid-March, 1939. The British response, with France in tow, was to draw a sort of chalk line across the map of Europe from the Baltic to the Black Sea and the Aegean and to announce that aggression beyond it would bring Britain and France to the side of the victim.[23]

[22] Notably from the United States and Russia.

[23] After an Anglo-French guarantee to Poland on March 31st, similar but unilateral guarantees by both countries were offered to Greece, Rumania, Turkey and Hungary, and negotiations began for an understanding with Russia.

Hitler either did not believe Chamberlain or believed that France and Britain were so divided externally and internally that their resistance would be slight. He startled the world by concluding a nonaggression pact with Russia on August 22nd. Then, after the usual agonizing preliminaries, he launched his armies against Poland on September 1, 1939. Great Britain, after making sure that her own ultimatum and American protests were being ignored, announced on September 3, 1939, that she was at war with Germany.

Many attempts have been made by Britons and non-Britons to explain the history of the fountainhead of the English-speaking peoples. Reflective Americans, in particular, have throughout their nation's existence thought and written much about the British tradition and the British institutions of freedom which they inherited and infused with their own powerful spirit and environment. A hundred years ago, Emerson, whose central aim it was to acquaint Americans with their nature and their highest potentialities, made two journeys of studious inspection to Britain and after long deliberation published his conclusions in *English Traits* (1856), a book of lively interest today. In one of the most fascinating brotherly exchanges on record, the American novelist Henry James, who became a British citizen, and William, the great psychologist, who remained almost aggressively American, each tried in vain to convince the other of his rightness. In 1914, the famous American philosopher, George Santayana, went to live in England, and he too tried to interpret her to Americans in his *Soliloquies in England* (1922).[24]

[24] He also tried to explain the American scene to Britons in his *Character and Opinion in the United States* (1920).

When there is added to such instances the almost continuous concern of thoughtful Americans over the interlocking of American and British foreign policies, it becomes obvious that Americans have never been able to ignore the role of Great Britain in the world and in their own lives, no matter how much they may have wanted to. The teasing problem has come back to puzzle them again and again since the parting took place in 1776. Americans have inevitably found much that was congenial and much to praise, but they have been restrained from wholesale commendation because they have been determined to differentiate their own from Britons' treatment of the common heritage from the past. The two peoples may have been evolving within the same general libertarian formula, nationally and internationally, but they have been compelled to give it different expressions.

Perhaps, therefore, as good a summary expression as any for Americans was uttered late in August, 1914, by John Jay Chapman, a brilliant and irascible fellow countryman of theirs. He had been trying in vain, publicly and privately, to persuade the British government to state its war aims. "The English don't understand the idea of acting for the world," he wrote in his diary. "To act for themselves with resultant benefit to the world—(because on the whole their methods were more liberal and gentler than those of any other nations). This has been their destiny." [25] In the earth's company of nations, none of which has yet dedicated itself to "acting for the world," that destiny is remarkably similar to the role which Americans like to think of as their own.

[25] M. A. D. Howe, *John Jay Chapman and His Letters* (Boston, 1937), pp. 284–5.

CHRONOLOGICAL TABLES

SOVEREIGNS

Alfred, 871–899
Edward, 899–924
Edgar, 959–975
Canute, 1017–1035
Edward, 1042–1066
Harold, 1066
William I, 1066–1087
William II, 1087–1100
Henry I, 1100–1135
Stephen, 1135–1154
Henry II, 1154–1189
Richard I, 1189–1199
John, 1199–1216
Henry III, 1216–1272
Edward I, 1272–1307
Edward II, 1307–1327
Edward III, 1327–1377
Richard II, 1377–1399
Henry IV, 1399–1413
Henry V, 1413–1422
Henry VI, 1422–1461
Edward IV, 1461–1483
Edward V, 1483

Richard III, 1483–1485
Henry VII, 1485–1509
Henry VIII, 1509–1547
Edward VI, 1547–1553
Mary, 1553–1558
Elizabeth, 1558–1603
James I, 1603–1625
Charles I, 1625–1649
Interregnum, 1649–1660
Charles II, 1660–1685
James II, 1685–1688
William III and Mary, 1689–1702
Anne, 1702–1714
George I, 1714–1727
George II, 1727–1760
George III, 1760–1820
George IV, 1820–1830
William IV, 1830–1837
Victoria, 1837–1901
Edward VII, 1901–1910
George V, 1910–1936
Edward VIII, 1936
George VI, 1936–

HEADS OF CABINETS

Sir Robert Walpole, 1721–1742
John Carteret, 1742–1744
Henry Pelham, 1744–1754
Duke of Newcastle, 1754–1756
William Pitt, 1756–1757

William Pitt and the Duke of Newcastle, 1757–1761
Duke of Newcastle and Lord Bute,
1761–1762
Lord Bute, 1762–1763

George Grenville, 1763–1765
Lord Rockingham, 1765–1766
William Pitt, Lord Chatham, 1766–1768
Duke of Grafton, 1768–1770
Lord North, 1770–1782
Lord Rockingham, 1782
Lord Shelburne, 1782–1783
Charles James Fox and Lord North, 1783
William Pitt, the Younger, 1783–1801
Henry Addington, 1801–1804
William Pitt, the Younger, 1804–1806
Charles James Fox, 1806–1807
Duke of Portland, 1807–1809
Spencer Perceval, 1809–1812
Lord Liverpool, 1812–1827
George Canning, 1827
Lord Goderich, 1827
Duke of Wellington, 1828–1830
Earl Grey, 1830–1834
Lord Melbourne, 1834
Sir Robert Peel, 1834–1835
Lord Melbourne, 1835–1841
Sir Robert Peel, 1841–1846
Lord John Russell, 1846–1852
Lord Derby and Benjamin Disraeli, 1852

Lord Aberdeen, 1852–1855
Lord Palmerston, 1855–1858
Lord Derby and Disraeli, 1858–1859
Lord Palmerston, 1859–1865
Lord Russell, 1865–1866
Lord Derby and Disraeli, 1866–1868
William Ewart Gladstone, 1868–1874
Disraeli, 1874–1880
Gladstone, 1880–1885
Lord Salisbury, 1885–1886
Gladstone, 1886
Lord Salisbury, 1886–1892
Gladstone, 1892–1894
Lord Rosebery, 1894–1895
Lord Salisbury, 1895–1902
Arthur James Balfour, 1902–1905
Sir Henry Campbell-Bannerman, 1905–1908
Herbert Henry Asquith, 1908–1916
David Lloyd George, 1916–1922
Andrew Bonar Law, 1922–1923
Stanley Baldwin, 1923–1924
James Ramsay MacDonald, 1924
Baldwin, 1924–1929
MacDonald, 1929–1931 (Labor); 1931–1935 (National)
Baldwin, 1935–1937
Neville Chamberlain, 1937–1940

SUGGESTIONS FOR FURTHER READING

The most authoritative detailed British histories are the *Oxford History of England,* edited by G. N. Clark, seven of whose projected fourteen volumes have appeared since 1934, and the *Cambridge History of the British Empire,* edited by J. H. Rose and others, seven of whose projected eight volumes have appeared since 1929. These works furnish guidance to special studies in all fields.

The best single-volume history by a British author, in spite of its slight treatment of recent times, is G. M. Trevelyan's *History of England* (1937). It may be interestingly supplemented by any of his more detailed works, notably his *English Social History* (1942). J. R. Green's *Short History of the English People* (4 vols., 1877–80), a colorful and sharply accented work which reflects an optimistic belief in progress, has deservedly retained broad popularity. Among British histories by Americans, W. E. Lunt's *History of England* (1938) is close-knit and comprehensive, and *A History of England and the British Empire,* by W. P. Hall and R. G. Albion (1937), is distinguished by its illustrative material and broad scope.

G. B. Adams's *Constitutional History of England,* as supplemented for recent years by R. L. Schuyler (1934), is the best single volume in its field. There is no satisfactory one-volume economic history. E. Lipson, *Economic History of England* (3 vols., 1934–37), coming down to 1800, and J. H. Clapham, *An Economic History of Modern Britain* (3 vols., 1926–38), ranging from 1820 to 1929, are the most useful larger works. N. S. B. and E. C. Gras give a remarkable panorama in their *Economic and Social History of an English Village, A.D. 909–1928* (1930). E. H. Legouis and L. Cazamian, in *A History of English Liter-*

ature (1935), profit by their detachment as French scholars, an advantage which is also evident in the several books by E. Halévy on British history since 1776. E. Wingfield-Stratford's *History of British Civilization* (1930) is a lively and independent interpretation.

There are separate biographies, ranging from indifferent to excellent, of practically all leading British figures, and brief biographical studies of thousands of individuals are to be found in the *Dictionary of National Biography* (63 vols., and supplements, 1885–1930). *Who's Who* is useful for contemporary figures.

The Annual Register has furnished each year since 1759 a running chronicle of British affairs.

Index

Books That Live

The Norton imprint on a book means that in the publisher's estimation it is a book not for a single season but for the years.

W · W · NORTON & CO · INC.
70 FIFTH AVENUE
NEW YORK